OJIBWE JOURNEYS
Treaties, Sandy Lake & The Waabanong Run

By Charlie Otto Rasmussen

Published by the Great Lakes Indian Fish & Wildlife Commission Press
72682 Maple Street
Odanah, WI 54861
715-682-6619

Second Printing, June 2011

Cover Photography: Charlie Otto Rasmussen
Layout Design: Stewart-Taylor Printing

Library of Congress Control Number: 2003090881

ISBN 0-9665820-2-0

Printed in the United States of America

To the Ojibweg who attended the 1850 Sandy Lake annuity payment and their families. Mikwendaagoziwag.

And Gene Connor, a selfless advocate for Ojibwe people. He is missed by his fellow runners.

CONTENTS

Notes on the text

Readers familiar with the terms Chippewa, Ojibwa, Ojibwe, Ojibway and Anishinaabe understand them to represent the same distinct group of American Indians living for the most part in the greater Lake Superior region. Over time, "Chippewa" has been used in a legal and political context, notably in nineteenth century treaties, and it still often appears in mainstream media publications. "Anishinaabe" has been increasingly favored as the term "the people" call themselves. Because Anishinaabe is popularly translated into English as "original people" or simply "Indian," I use Ojibwe throughout to avoid any confusion with other indigenous groups except when used in a proper title (e.g. Ojibways of Onigaming).

In accordance with Ojibwemowin (the Ojibwe language), readers will notice the letter "g" is used to pluralize Ojibwe words (e.g. Ojibweg). The reference book, *A Concise Dictionary of Minnesota Ojibwe,* by John Nichols and Earl Nyholm serves as a guide for most Ojibwe spellings. Ojibwe words are italicized the first time they appear in the narrative.

Finally, the words "band" and "tribe" are used interchangeably to indicate organized, identifiable Indian communities.

Foreword

Billy Mills
Oglala Sioux

As I read *Ojibwe Journeys: Treaties, Sandy Lake and the Waabanong Run*, my thoughts raced back to October 14, 1964 when I won the Gold Medal in the Olympic Games 10,000 meter run. As I circled the Olympic track in Tokyo, Japan, I was reminded how in the old days we ran to draw strength from the four directions, from Mother Earth and from our Creator—all to prepare us for the challenges we would face now and later in life. Perhaps this is why running always takes me on a journey to the center of my soul, challenging my integrity, my character and strengthening my humility, all the while empowering me spiritually.

Ojibwe Journeys reconfirmed in me how the signing of our treaties with the United States government was our defining moment as nations. They changed our social and economic fabric. The journey to Sandy Lake in 1850 speaks graphically of how we as tribal people must hold to the legal fact and precedent that the signing of our treaties with the United States government was, and still is, legal and sacred.

The story of the Waabanong Run and 93-year-old Chief Buffalo making the journey to Washington D.C., paddling a quarter of the way in a canoe to defend tribal treaty rights, speaks volumes, and so eloquently, of the sacrifice, pain and determination many have gone through to defend our legal and human rights all the while envisioning a better world for our children.

The reading of *Ojibwe Journeys* articulates to my heart and soul that we must continue to meet our changing world by holding the

United States government to its legal and moral obligations of implementing and delivering its treaty responsibilities to Indian nations.

If lessons can be learned, consider these: First, there is a glaring need for the United States to pursue global unity through accepting the dignity, character and beauty of diversity. It is the future of human kind. Second, the primary downfall with our American free enterprise system is profit at all costs. Lastly, Indian nations must articulate in a precise, compassionate, compelling manner our vision for the future. We must continually work on designing an infrastructure for the implementation and delivery of treaty responsibilities. The Great Lakes Indian Fish & Wildlife Commission is but one example of how that can be done. We need intelligent and adaptive programs of change, like a mandated study of Indian history in primary schools and the incorporation of Indian law into the curriculum of future attorneys.

We seek all this while strengthening our cultural, traditional and spiritual values. Like the Waabanong Run, blending law and spirituality as runners sacrificed themselves on a journey through the heartland of America and joined with legal experts on steps of the U.S. Supreme Court. They were encouraged to go forward with the words "each step is a prayer." Through prayer, sacrifice and understanding there can be justice.

Ojibwe Journeys reminds me that it is a good day to run.

INTRODUCTION

Driving wind and snow rocked the long passenger van I steered toward the Lac du Flambeau reservation in northeast Wisconsin. Tall evergreen trees, vaguely seen in the clash of white whipping snow and evening darkness, bent violently over the road. On the airwaves Gordon Lightfoot's epic, "The Wreck of the *Edmund Fitzgerald*," crackled through the late autumn storm and seemed to find its way onto every local radio station. Twenty-three years earlier the "*Fitz*," an iron ore freighter, sank with its crew into Lake Superior in similar, more severe, conditions.

Anniversaries are important ways human beings remember people and events of the past; they help us understand who we are as individuals, communities and distinct ethnic groups. For other reasons this was a night of reflection for people in the upper Great Lakes region. Elsewhere on the highways to Lac du Flambeau, a handful of travelers bucked against the storm to assemble at the reservation to learn, receive and participate in traditional teachings of Ojibwe Indian people.

On this occasion, there was no calendar anniversary to draw them together, rather a familiar threat to the lifestyle and identity of the Ojibwe had mounted a formidable challenge. In a short time, the United States Supreme Court would render a verdict on the status of Ojibwe rights to harvest traditional resources from territory in Minnesota—a decision that could also affect other Indian people across the nation. Seeking council of Ojibwe spiritual leaders and elders, people gathered at Lac du Flambeau in preparation for the Waabanong Run. The elders who knew—who remembered—the spiritual ways that utilize sage, tobacco, prayer and song would prepare runners for the one-thousand-mile journey to Washington DC; there, on December 2, 1998, the High Court would hear arguments in the *Minnesota v. Mille Lacs* case.

Unknown to scheduling managers for the Supreme Court, December 2 represented a little-recognized but particularly significant anniversary. On that day 148 years earlier, a famished and ill group of Ojibwe Indians were issued the remaining cache of rotten food and some dry goods from government agents at Sandy Lake, Minnesota Territory while hundreds of their dead and dying relatives lay scattered for miles. The plan hatched by a group of government officials that brought the Ojibweg there had seemed simple enough: switch the treaty annuity payment site from the centrally-located Madeline Island to Sandy Lake. If Wisconsin and Upper Michigan Ojibweg wanted the money and goods (annuities) due to them for ceding tribal lands to the United States, they had no choice but to make the long journey west. Indian agents might then convince the large Ojibwe population to stay and take up residence, creating an economic boon for the region with a flood of federal money to administer Indian programs. The plan hinged on winter weather preventing the Ojibweg from canoeing home—up to 500 water miles. The annuity payment was delayed by six weeks, and infectious disease tore through their ranks while the Ojibweg waited at Sandy Lake. Snow and ice soon gripped the land.

Sandy Lake, however, was already home to a band of Ojibwe who made a tenuous living from the land. The eastern tribes had little desire to stay there. They wanted to return to their own homes south of Lake Superior. After all, in land cession treaties signed several years earlier, tribal leaders insisted on keeping the right to live off the land where they were raised—the land that protected the graves of their ancestors. So they wrapped their dead in birch bark along the shores of Sandy Lake and trudged homeward to the east. And people kept dying.

Anniversaries have a way of converging through the years. Names and faces changed between December 2, 1850 and 1998, but one goal of the Ojibwe antagonists remained the same: to eliminate the legal rights the Ojibweg reserved in the territory ceded in 1837.

The quest to defend those rights has led the Ojibweg on a long and winding trail. Ever since the practice of hunting, fishing and gathering was reserved on ceded lands, Ojibwe people have embarked on a journey to protect those reserved rights from opposing forces. Those journeys unfolded over time and across the earth as Ojibweg traveled great distances on ventures that were driven by spirituality, cultural survival and love for the land. This volume attempts to trace those journeys and demonstrate deeper meaning to the lifeway and history of Ojibwe people in the greater Lake Superior region of the United States.

It has been my privilege to chronicle and participate in recent Ojibwe journeys that appear in the following pages. Text in Chapters Three through Five include my first-hand observations which oftentimes appear without a footnote. Information in earlier chapters is largely an extension of my graduate studies at the University of Wisconsin—Eau Claire and based on the work of academics, primary sources and interviews I conducted over the past few years.

Chi miigwech to all my colleagues and coworkers who contributed comments and thoughtful advice on the text. And to the Aitkin County Historical Society, Minnesota Historical Society, Northeast Minnesota History Center, Vaughn Library (Ashland), Wisconsin Historical Society, Esteban Chiriboga, Steve White and Jonathan Gilbert for their timely attention to graphic, photo and information requests.

Charlie Otto Rasmussen
Odanah, Wisconsin
January 2003

Ojibwe Country circa 1850: Western Lake Superior

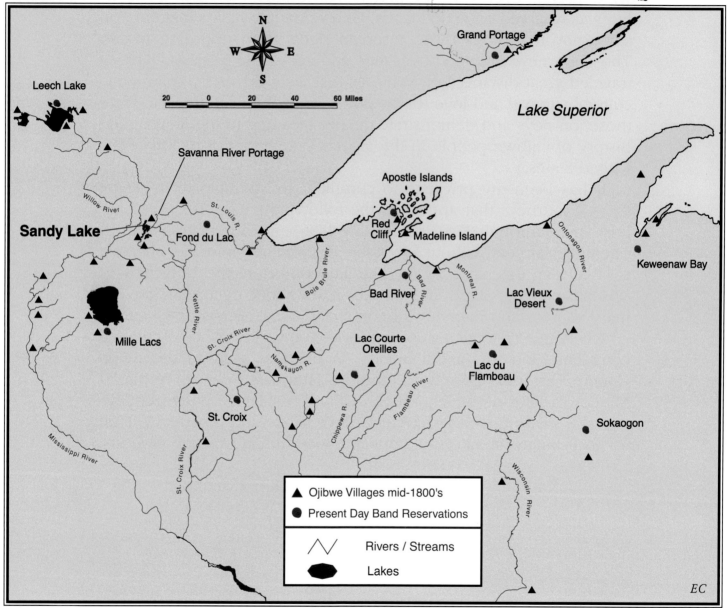

Leech Lake

Savanna River Portage

Willow River

Sandy Lake

Fond du Lac

St. Louis R.

Lake Superior

Grand Portage

Apostle Islands

Red Cliff

Madeline Island

Kettle River

Bois Brule River

Bad River

Bad River

Montreal R.

Ontonagon River

Keweenaw Bay

Lac Vieux Desert

Mille Lacs

St. Croix River

Namekagon R.

Lac Courte Oreilles

Chippewa R.

Flambeau River

Lac du Flamboau

Sokaogon

Mississippi River

St. Croix River

St. Croix

Wisconsin River

▲ Ojibwe Villages mid-1800's

● Present Day Band Reservations

/\ Rivers / Streams

⬛ Lakes

EC

"When the order to move came, Chief Buffalo sent runners out in all directions to seek for reasons and causes for the order, but all those men returned without finding a single reason among the Superior and Mississippi Indians why the great father had become displeased."

Benjamin Armstrong, 1892

CHAPTER ONE:
Formative Journeys

For more than 150 years following the arrival of Europeans in the Lake Superior region, Ojibwe Indians maintained relative autonomy from French and later British colonial authorities. Although missionaries scoured Indian villages on a campaign to convert local tribes from their traditional religion to Christianity, Europeans were primarily interested in sustaining the lucrative fur trade that began here in the 1650s. Fundamental Ojibwe culture and lifestyles remained largely intact as only a handful of forts and trading posts penetrated the vast wild land.

The United States government, however, had different designs for Ojibwe Country. It came seeking the remaining fur, then the trees, mineral resources, land and ultimately sought to take away the very identity of Indian people. While many federal and state government efforts did effectively tear into the heart of Ojibwe culture, the people maintained a quiet resilience.[1] An important journey lay ahead.

Michitweg and early Ojibwe runners

In the centuries before the construction of roads and high-wire communication lines, runners served a vital role in Ojibwe communities across the upper Great Lakes region. Both men and women, known as michitweg, were messengers who traveled between population centers via woodland trails, lakes and rivers. Elders passed the running tradition onto their children and grandchildren, fostering a legacy that spanned generations in some families.[2]

Michitweg of the deep northern forests needed more than a good pair of moccasins (makizinan) as long distance travel sometimes meant toting a birch bark canoe to utilize the waterways where Ojibwe villages were usually located. To improve performance and feel "light footed," some nineteenth century Ojibwe walked around with narrow bags containing lead shot strapped to their ankles prior to running. As snow accumulated

Many remarkable performances of the Indian runners are generally known. They can cover an extraordinary space of ground by their persistent and steady trot. As the sparse population of the country is scattered over wide distances, cases frequently occur in which a swift runner can save a family from destruction; and this is a sufficient reason why the [Ojibwe] honour him as greatly as a bold hunter or warrior.

Johann Georg Kohl, 1855

Ojibwe hunters and messengers *wore snowshoes in the winter.* GLIFWC

Dakota warriors attack Ojibwe positions on the east shore of the Bois Brule River in northwest Wisconsin around 1841. WHI (X3) 24687

and water routes froze over in the winter, the michitweg relied on snowshoes for overland travel.[3]

When a person fell ill without a qualified healer available, the michitweg were summoned. Attended by tobacco *(asemaa)*, ceremony and prayer, an individual was asked to journey through the expansive northern forest to contact healers in other villages. Such excursions ranged from a few dozen miles to well over one hundred miles, requiring the michitweg to pass through other Indian communities. Runners were held in high esteem and received support from Ojibwe people along the way, including food and lodging. On long journeys that passed through multiple Ojibwe villages, local michitweg helped carry messages down the trail, creating an intertribal relay system.[4]

Intermittent tension between the Dakota and Ojibweg from the seventeenth century through the mid-nineteenth century, however, loomed over these urgent treks through the northwoods. During fair weather months, Ojibwe and Dakota war parties battled for control of trapping, hunting and gathering areas along the western edge of Ojibwe territory, known as the "war road." This perennial skirmish line generally followed the division between prairie and forest vegetation zones—from Wisconsin's lower Chippewa River, northwest through the headwaters of the Mississippi River, and onto Lake of the Woods in far northern Minnesota.[5] Despite the hostilities, the michitweg were often exempt from harm as they passed through enemy territory. Like American Indian runners in some West Coast tribes, the michitweg were recognized for their venerable responsibilities, enjoying the privilege of safe passage.[6]

As tribes began incorporating European economics into their livelihood, Ojibwe runners found employment as postmen for French and English fur companies located in the Lake Superior *(Gichi Gami)* region. After America claimed this territory—known as the Northwest—the U.S. Postal Service recruited Ojibwe men to transport mail by dogsled across the frozen land. Grand Portage

Ojibwe John Beargrease gained notoriety from his mail delivery exploits by land and sea along the north shore of Lake Superior in the late 1800s. Around the same time, northwest Wisconsin Ojibwe Antoine Dennis made biweekly mail runs between Superior and Bayfield, covering more than thirty miles a day on foot. Carrying a 70-pound mail pack supported by a strap across his forehead, Dennis traveled the woodland route for nearly six years and wore snowshoes in winter.[7]

Some Ojibwe communities living north of Lake Superior in Canada utilized runners well into the twentieth century as good roads and telephone lines were slow to reach isolated villages.[8]

Treaty making in Ojibwe Country

More than two hundred years have passed since American, Ojibwe and other Indian representatives met to negotiate the Treaty of 1785 in western Pennsylvania. The 1785 Treaty was the first of 42 treaties between the U.S. and various Ojibwe nations, laying the foundation for later land cessions and, in effect, Ojibwe treaty rights. For the United States government, treaties were an opportune means of defining the boundaries of American Indian nations to orchestrate land acquisitions for settlement and access to natural resources. A decade later in the Treaty of 1795 at Greenville, the U.S. recognized indigenous bands as sovereign nations in Minnesota, Wisconsin and Upper Michigan.[9]

In the western Great Lakes, where vast contiguous forests and rugged terrain dominated the landscape, there was little interest in American settlement. Ojibwe, Potawatomi, Menominee and other indigenous people lived a subsistence lifestyle of seasonal hunting, fishing, gathering and limited agriculture supplemented by European goods acquired from fur traders.

As the United States expanded westward in the early nineteenth century, raw materials used to fuel the country's rapid growth came under short supply. The Ojibwe territory of the Lake Superior region was rich in important resources like pine timber, copper and iron ore, and government officials maneuvered to gain title to Indian lands.

The Treaty of 1825 at Prairie du Chien was instrumental in setting up Ojibwe land cessions over the next three decades. Dakota and Ojibwe bands were the foremost participants in the treaty that did not include property transfers, but recognized Indian title to the land and established tribal boundaries across present-day Wisconsin and Minnesota.[10]

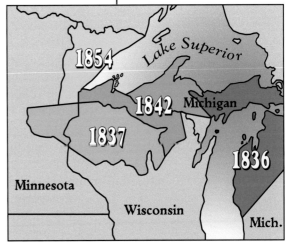

Ojibwe land ceded to the United States through the Treaties of 1836, 1837, 1842 and 1854.

The need for timber to build towns in Middle America became more pronounced over the following years, and in 1837 the government sought access to the mighty red and white pine forests occupied by the Ojibweg. Wisconsin Territorial Governor Henry Dodge petitioned Ojibwe representatives to gather at the confluence of the Minnesota and Mississippi Rivers near Fort Snelling in late July. With tribal boundaries neatly in place from the earlier treaty, government officials bargained for 13 million acres of Ojibwe land, from Mole Lake, Wisconsin to Mille Lacs, Minnesota. Known as the Pine Tree Treaty, the Ojibwe made the transaction contingent on retaining their rights to hunt, fish and gather in the newly ceded territory.[11]

Ojibwe and United States officials met five years later in 1842 to negotiate the sale of an additional 10 million acres of land in the Lake Superior region. Here again, Ojibwe leaders insisted on retaining the right to live off the land, following the traditional harvest cycle that centered on wild plants, maple syrup, fish and game.[12]

In addition to harvesting rights on the land, tribal beneficiaries of the 1837 and 1842 Treaties were entitled to annuity payments spread over 20-25 years. Annuity compensation was intended to cover the purchase price of the land and generally included cash, food, tobacco and everyday utility items like blankets.[13]

Tell [Ramsey] I blame him for the children we have lost, for the sickness we have suffered, and for the hunger we have endured. The fault rests on his shoulders.

Flat Mouth,
Leech Lake Ojibwe,
Dec. 3, 1850 [14]

Sandy Lake, Minnesota

The promises spoken at the Treaties of 1837 and 1842 were still fresh in the northern air when band members learned that some government officials were devising a plan to push them westward. Seeking the economic benefits of a large Indian population in the Minnesota Territory, Governor and Superintendent of Indian Affairs in Minnesota, Alexander Ramsey, worked with other officials to remove the Ojibweg from their homes in Wisconsin and Upper Michigan westward to Sandy Lake. The flow of annuity money and government funds to build Indian schools, agencies and farms would create wealth for Ramsey and provide salaried positions for his supporters in Minnesota. Patronage—appointing federal jobs to loyal followers—was an important step in controlling the territories' political machinery.[15]

Pressured by Ramsey and others, United States President Zachary Taylor issued an executive order in February 1850 that sought to move Ojibwe Indians living east of the Mississippi River to their unceded lands. It wasn't the first occasion Taylor endorsed removing Wisconsin Indians. As a former U.S. military commander, Taylor played a key role in driving Sauk Indians from southwest Wisconsin 18 years earlier during the bloody campaign against Black Hawk's band of one thousand men, women and children.[16]

Ojibwe chiefs responded to Taylor's order by calling upon the michitweg to tour every village and determine if Indian people were in conflict with any of the 500 white settlers who resided in the Lake Superior region. Tribal leaders understood from earlier treaty negotiations that removal from the ceded territory might only occur if the Ojibwe made war against whites. To the contrary, Ojibwe-settler relations were considered very good and a broad-based coalition of white interests, from missionary groups, newspapers, and even Wisconsin state legislators, rallied to oppose the Removal Order.[17]

Despite staunch support for the Ojibwe to remain in their homelands, Ramsey and his subordinate, Indian Sub-agent John Watrous, were resolved; more Ojibwe people in Minnesota meant a greater flow of federal money and goods in the form of annuity payments. Most Wisconsin and Upper Michigan Ojibwe bands collected treaty annuity payments at La Pointe on Madeline Island, near their principal villages. The spiritual hub of the Ojibwe nations, Madeline Island was both sacred ground and a convenient gathering place for a majority of the tribes.

Hoping to entice these eastern Ojibweg to Minnesota Territory, the Office of Indian Affairs directed tribal members to Sandy Lake in October 1850 to receive their annuities. By moving the distribution site several hundred miles west, Ramsey and Watrous planned to trap the Ojibweg over the coming winter and compel them to take up residence in Minnesota.[18]

While tribal members from Michigan and some eastern reaches of Wisconsin refused to travel with winter fast approaching, approximately 5,500 Ojibweg journeyed to Sandy Lake that autumn. They

This unlooked for order has brought disappointment and consternation to the Indians throughout the Lake Superior Country, and will bring upon them the most disastrous consequences.

Lake Superior News and Mining Journal, June 12, 1850

Ojibwe artist Aindibitunk created this sketch of La Pointe on Madeline Island in the mid-1800s for the United States Geological Survey. WHI (X3) 25367

The annuity payment at the Sandy Lake Indian Sub-agency in 1850 was delayed by six weeks causing suffering for thousands of Ojibwe Indians, and led to the loss of hundreds of lives. FK

arrived in waves around the payment date, fatigued and hungry, only to find that Watrous was away in St. Louis, and the payments would be delayed. Wild game was scarce; fishing was poor, and high water had wiped out the wild rice crop for the second consecutive year. For the weary travelers and those Ojibweg who resided at Sandy Lake, living conditions deteriorated rapidly.[19]

Over a six-week period as harsh winter conditions set in, band members waited near the newly established Indian sub-agency situated near the northwest shoreline. Government workers eventually issued the Ojibweg small rations of river-soaked flour and pork from tribal annuity stocks. Yet even the starving Ojibweg found that the rotten food "was so much damaged that [they] could not eat it." Without adequate food or shelter, disease and exposure ravaged the Ojibwe families. Ultimately, more than 150 died at Sandy Lake from complications caused by dysentery and measles.[20]

A partial annuity payment was finally completed on December 2, providing the Ojibweg with a meager three-day food supply and no cash to buy desperately needed provisions at trading posts on the trail home. The following day most of the Ojibweg broke camp, while a handful stayed behind to care for approximately 200 people too ill to travel. With over a foot of snow on the ground and the waterways frozen over, Ojibwe families walked hundreds of miles to get back home.[21]

Even those facing a comparatively short homeward journey (60 miles) were not spared from the suffering. A missionary's wife related the brutal experience of one family returning to Leech Lake after the annuity payment:

> *Three days' march from Leech Lake, the two children were taken sick, the oldest a boy of twelve years old. The father was obliged to carry his sick son, and the mother the daughter, until the last night before they reached Leech Lake, when the boy died. The next morning they set off again, the father carrying the corpse of his son, and the mother a sick child. About noon the girl died, but they came on until they reached Leech Lake, bringing the dead bodies of their children on their backs.*
>
> *Red Lake, Minn., February 1851*[22]

Some 250 people died on those bitter trails, and the Ojibweg vowed never to abandon their villages in Wisconsin and Upper Michigan for Sandy Lake.

Through the winter and spring of 1851, news of the Sandy Lake annuity debacle spread eastward from the Lake Superior region. Newspapers from Sault Ste. Marie, Cleveland and New York City amplified general public displeasure in government removal plans for the Ojibweg. Pressured by the growing volume of petitions from members of the Wisconsin Legislature, missionaries, businessmen and other ceded territory residents, Commissioner of Indian Affairs Luke Lea suspended the Removal Order in the summer of 1851.[23]

The deaths of some 400 tribal members, widespread opposition to removal and Lea's suspension left Ramsey and Watrous undeterred, and they redoubled their efforts, insisting that the Lake Superior Ojibweg remove to Sandy Lake. Government advisors, like farmers, blacksmiths and carpenters assigned to assist Indian communities, were withdrawn from service. Watrous halted crop planting in the fields at Bad River and ordered tribal members to Minnesota, or risk the arrival of soldiers to force their departure. After receiving persuasive reports from Ramsey and Watrous in November, Commissioner Lea decided the Ojibweg should be removed after all for "humanitarian reasons" and reinstated the order. If the Ojibweg hoped to receive anything guaranteed in the 1837 and 1842 Treaties, they were required to abandon their homes south of Lake Superior.[24]

Buffalo challenges removal

As government leaders worked to circumvent both the treaties and public sentiment, Chief Buffalo *(Bizhiki)* of La Pointe and other Ojibwe headmen dictated a letter in the fall of 1851 to Commissioner Lea protesting the attempted removal to Sandy Lake and charged Agent Watrous with carrying out a "great deception towards [the Ojibwe]." Hoping to put an end to the depraved removal schemes, the chiefs requested an audience with American leaders in Washington DC.[25]

By ice-out the following spring, Ojibwe leaders were growing restless; there was still no response from Commissioner Lea regarding their petition. Well into his 90s, the aged Buffalo had waited long enough and set out for the long

An Ojibwe healer attempts to cure an ailing man. A handful of eastern Ojibwe stayed at Sandy Lake over the winter of 1850-51 to care for around 200 people too sick to travel home. WHI (X3) 25390

Buffalo's party takes refuge from a storm along the south shore of Lake Superior on their journey to Washington DC. WHI (X3) 24685

U. S. President Millard Fillmore

journey east, from Madeline Island to Washington on April 5, 1852, with Chief Oshoga, white interpreter Benjamin Armstrong and four additional Ojibwe headmen. Traveling from the village of La Pointe in a 24-foot birch bark canoe, the delegation worked their way along the south shore of Lake Superior, camping at the mouth of the Montreal River on the first evening. Their provisions were few, consisting of crackers, sugar and coffee; wild game and fish were harvested along the way. Stops at Ontonagon, Houghton, Hancock and Marquette afforded Armstrong the opportunity to circulate a petition that supported the Ojibwe cause. Merchants, lumbermen and copper miners endorsed the document with "a great many signatures."[26]

The petition intended for President Millard Fillmore proclaimed that "while [Ojibwe] removal West would in Our Opinion be a great damage to them it would in no manner benefit the white population of the Country."[27] While local residents may have had a genuine interest in the welfare of the Ojibwe, the small American population of Lake Superior's south shore was financially inclined to retain these Indian communities which provided labor to logging and mining industries and bolstered the region's economy through their annuities.

Battling severe storms that at times forced them ashore, the party canoed as far as Sault Ste. Marie, Michigan, an historic crossroads known to the Ojibwe as *Boweting*. From there, they traveled aboard the steamship *Northerner* through Lakes Huron and St. Clair before docking at Detroit. Crossing the full length of Lake Erie, they came to Buffalo, New York where they boarded a train bound for Albany. After sailing on yet another steamer to New York City, followed by an overland leg, they reached their destination.[28]

Upon arriving in Washington DC after the 10-week journey, Commissioner Lea told Armstrong that he and the Ojibwe must return home since they had not been invited. By chance, New York Congressman George Briggs and members of Fillmore's staff met the Ojibwe delegation while dining. Impressed by Buffalo and his companions, the bureaucrats helped arrange a meeting with President Fillmore.[29]

With additional U.S. government officials in attendance, Fillmore received the group from La Pointe the following day. Buffalo began the meeting with a ceremony, using a pipe constructed explicitly for use with the President. After all had smoked, Oshoga, who was the principal orator, explained how Ojibwe leaders understood the terms of the 1837 and 1842 Treaties—most notably that they would never be required to leave their homelands as long as they maintained peaceful relations with white settlers. Armstrong translated Oshoga's lengthy speech and presented the President with the petition supporting the Ojibwe.[30]

After thoughtful consideration, Fillmore recalled Buffalo's delegation to the White House several days later to render his decision: the Removal Order would be countermanded and annuity payments would return to La Pointe.[31]

Satisfied with the President's assurances, the Ojibweg and Armstrong boarded a train for the journey home. They traveled by rail until reaching LaCrosse, Wis., where the delegation transferred onto a steamboat and chugged their way up the Mississippi River to St. Paul. Then striking out on an "Indian trail across the country to Lake Superior," Buffalo's party returned home, sharing the good news of President Fillmore's decision with Ojibwe people along the way.[32]

Treaty rights and the rise of state game laws

As American territories were organized into states through the nineteenth century, many newly formed legislatures enacted laws to protect wild game populations from unchecked market hunting. White-tailed deer, ducks and fish were slaughtered by market hunters and shipped by wagon and later trainload to feed the inhabitants of growing cities. Incoming settlers, sportsmen and hunters who supplied meat to mining and timber camps, further depleted game populations.

To the dismay of tribal members in the 1837 and 1842 ceded territories, however, wardens began imposing state game laws on Ojibwe hunters and fishermen. While there was little enforcement of these laws until the 1890s, state officials progressively sought to curtail Ojibwe treaty harvests over the next century.

One year after an 1836 treaty with Ottawa and Ojibwe tribes, Michigan became a state. But hunting and fishing restrictions didn't appear until 1859, prohibiting the harvest of deer, wild turkey and woodcock during their respective breeding cycles. Nearly 30 years later, game wardens were employed to enforce a series of laws passed by the state through the later half of the nineteenth century.[33]

When the United States sought tribal land in Minnesota's Arrowhead region several years after the failed removal attempt, the Ojibweg of the Lake Superior region agreed to cede more territory in exchange for permanent reservations in Upper Michigan and Wisconsin through the Treaty of 1854. Driven by the events at Sandy Lake and a love for the homeland and graves of their forefathers, these Ojibweg were resolved to stay in their traditional villages and continue their hunting and gathering lifestyle. The establishment of homeland reservations marked the end of federal efforts to remove them west of the Mississippi River.

Buffalo's delegation to Washington DC in 1852. White interpreter Benjamin Armstrong appears in the upper right corner. *WHI (D485) 6264*

When Minnesota attained statehood in 1858, lawmakers enacted statutes establishing hunting seasons for deer, elk and game birds like grouse and prairie chickens. Enforcement of game laws did not occur until 1892, however, and even then, only random incidents involving tribal members were reported in local newspapers.[34]

An 1868 Wisconsin law recognized that Ojibwe Indians were exempt from state game laws within reservation boundaries, but it ignored ceded territory harvest rights. Eleven years later, Ashland, Bayfield and Douglas Counties hired wardens to enforce fish and game laws that set hunting, fishing and trapping seasons. By the 1890s, state game wardens joined county wardens and local sheriffs empowered to enforce game regulations, and treaty harvesters watched their ability to harvest off-reservation resources steadily deteriorate.[35]

At the turn of the century, a vast majority of the northern forest had been razed, and second-growth deciduous trees sprouted through the cutover land replacing the mighty pine forest. This dramatic habitat alteration had a mixed effect on Ojibwe subsistence lifestyle. The new forest composition provided excellent browse for white-tailed deer. Coupled with state regulations curbing market hunting, deer numbers increased, and the herd expanded their primary range further north. Water quality suffered, however, from immense river log drives and rainwater swept soil into waterways from the denuded land, affecting wild rice, plants and fish habitat.[36]

Despite government efforts to mold the semi-nomadic Ojibwe into sedentary farmers, agriculture played a limited role in Ojibwe subsistence during this period. While small gardens were common, most reservation land was ill suited for extensive agriculture, and the growing season was short, prompting tribal members to further diversify their economic pursuits. Employment with white businesses supplemented dwindling gains from traditional hunting, fishing and gathering. Ojibwe men found work as lumberjacks, miners and guides for urban sportsmen.[37]

For much of the twentieth century, policies enacted by state officials in Madison made off-reservation harvesting progressively more difficult—and costly. Tribal members served jail time, forfeited hunting rifles, paid fines, and even experienced car impoundments for exercising their reserved rights. Wisconsin attorneys with Ojibwe ancestry, like E. Ward Winton and Thomas L. St. Germaine, challenged state jurisdiction of natural resources from the 1910s to 30s and argued with little success that the federal treaties prevailed over other state laws.[38]

Tribal members in the Mille Lacs, Minnesota area seeking wild game off-reservation were also targeted by state officials. Under the cover of night, the Ojibweg shot deer with the aid of spotlights and netted walleye, storing the catch in underground pits. While the courts ordered fines and incarcerations, prosecuting tribal members proved difficult at times. Ojibweg who did not speak English required assistance from state-funded interpreters, and cases were sometimes dismissed by local judges unable to flesh out discrepancies between state and federal law.[39]

The push to impose state jurisdiction over natural resources in the ceded territory was further spurred by the blooming vacation industry. Railroads, followed by a system of northbound highways, funneled urban sightseers, fishermen and hunters to the lake country of Upper Michigan, Wisconsin and Minnesota beginning in the 1890s. Fish and game became a lucrative commercial commodity, and under the direction of state policymakers, wardens worked to eliminate competition from tribal subsistence harvesters. By the middle of the twentieth century, tourism was one of Wisconsin's largest industries as the surging

Dairy farm at Bad River, 1914. *Small family farms replaced forest land on some Ojibwe reservations under the direction of federal officials. Farming the cutover proved difficult, however, and tribal members relied on traditional resources and employment with white businesses to subsist. BRPL*

23

Sportsmen in Aitkin, Minn. after a successful hunt for moose and deer. Under the direction of state officials, game wardens cracked down on treaty-reserved hunting and fishing across the ceded territories as tourists entered the region in the early 1900s. ACHS

demand for resort lodging, restaurants, service stations, and sporting goods pumped millions of dollars into the state's economy.[40]

Gripped by poverty and widespread unemployment in the northwoods, many Ojibweg had little choice but to risk prosecution for breaching state hunting and fishing laws in order to feed their families. Reservation deer populations were under intense pressure and inadequate to meet the nutritional and ceremonial needs of tribal members. Considered "violators" by state officials, the cat-and-mouse game played out by the Ojibweg and game wardens continued into the 1970s when a series of court cases constructed a modern foundation for the exercise of treaty-reserved rights in the ceded territory.[41]

Notes: Chapter One

[1] See Edmund Danziger, *The Chippewas of Lake Superior* (Norman: University of Oklahoma Press) and Richard White, *The Middle Ground: Indians, Empires and Republics in the Great Lakes Region, 1650-1815* (Cambridge University Press) for more discussion on how Indians and whites interacted over time.
[2] Tobasonakwut Kinew interview.
[3] Robert Bieder. *Kitchi Gami*, 122; Peter Nabokov. *Indian Running*, 86.
[4] Kinew interview; Bieder, 122.
[5] William W. Warren. *History of the Ojibway People*; Helen Hornbeck Tanner. *Atlas of Great Lakes Indian History*; 65; Warren Upham, *Minnesota Place Names,* 3rd ed. rev., p.511.
[6] Kinew; Nabokov, 16-17.
[7] Bieder, 122; Charles E. Cleland. *Place of the Pike,* 45; Arthur Tenny Holbrook, "Antoine Dennis," 379-382.

[8] Kinew.

[9] Institute for the Development of Indian Law, "Treaties and Agreements of the Chippewa Indians." The term "treaty rights" refers to specific conditions Ojibwe leaders required in the Treaties of 1836, 1837, 1842, and 1854. The continued privilege to hunt, fish and gather wild plants off-reservation are common treaty rights.

[10] Ronald Satz. *Chippewa Treaty Rights,* 6.

[11] Satz, 13.

[12] Ibid, 39.

[13] Ibid, 155, 172.

[14] Mark Diedrich. *Ojibway Oratory,* 48.

[15] James A. Clifton. "Wisconsin Death March," 20.

[16] Satz, 53; Nancy Oestreich Lurie. *Wisconsin Indians,* 18; Elbert Smith. *The Presidencies of Zachary Taylor and Millard Fillmore,* 29.

[17] Benjamin Armstrong. "Reminiscences of Life Among the Chippewas," 297; Satz, 55-56.

[18] Clifton, 23.

[19] Annuity Roll, Nov. 28, 1850, Chippewa Annuity Rolls from National Archives and Records Service; Bruce White. "The Regional Context of the Removal Order of 1850," 194; Edmund J. Danziger. *The Chippewas of Lake Superior,* 80. Watrous estimated that 4,000 Ojibweg attended the 1850 annuity payment at Sandy Lake. The annuity roll, however, indicates that nearly 5,400 Ojibwe received annuities following the deadly six week delay. While it is unclear whether heads-of-families were allowed to collect annuities for those who did not attend, scholars and primary sources suggest that entire families were, indeed, on hand for the payment. Furthermore, since the plan was to remove eastern Ojibweg to Minnesota, local Indian Agents would logically have coerced whole families to make the journey.

[20] *Aitken Independent Age:* Sept. 27, 2000, "Brief and Tragic History of the Sandy Lake Indian Agency," 3; John Pitezel. *Lights and Shades of Missionary Life,* 299; Armstrong, 292; White, 192.

[21] White, 192-93.

[22] Neil, Rev. Edward D. *The History of Minnesota,* 550-51.

[23] Satz, 61-62.

[24] Satz, 62; Armstrong, 291.

[25] Buffalo to Lea, Nov. 6, 1851 in US Dist. Court, 226.

[26] Armstrong, 293.

[27] Satz, 64.

[28] Armstrong, 293-296.

[29] Ibid.

[30] Armstrong, 297; Danziger, 89; Tim Pfaff. *Paths of the People,* 36.

[31] Armstrong, 298.

[32] Ibid.

[33] Michigan DNR, "Landmark Dates."

[34] *Mille Lacs v. Minnesota,* 861 F. Supp. 784, (D.Minn 1994), p. 820-821.

[35] *LCO v. Wisconsin,* Deposition of James Pipe Mustache, 1990; James Oberly. *The Lake Superior Chippewas and Treaty Rights in the Ceded Territory of Wisconsin,* 81, 85.

[36] Oberly, 54.

[37] Satz, 72.

[38] E. Ward Winton. "Memoirs of Ward Winton: Legal Battles in Behalf of the Lac Court[e] Oreilles Band of Chippewa Indians of Wisconsin, 1972," 47; Satz, 87; Oberly, 95-116.

[39] Buffalohead, 89-90.

[40] Charles E. Cleland. *Rites of Conquest,* 280; Nesbit, 514, 528; Buffalohead, 102.

[41] Mike Tribble interview.

CHAPTER TWO:
Gichi Gami and the Wisconsin Mainland

For more than 70 years, the Ojibweg of the Lake Superior region were forced to exercise their off-reservation treaty rights in secrecy, often paying a high price to the states that targeted them as criminals. It is a period sometimes remembered in colorful stories of tribal members dodging overzealous wardens; in most cases, however, state harassment of off-reservation harvesters simply exacerbated the problems of malnourishment, poor living conditions, unemployment, and inadequate health care in Ojibwe communities. It was, in fact, a dark time for many American Indians. But widespread social changes circulating across the United States provided a spark in the late 1960s, breathing new life into the treaty journey.[1]

On the heels of the black struggle for equality in the South and a counterculture rejection of mainstream American life and the Vietnam War, American Indians began mobilizing in order to address grievances that had simmered throughout the 1960s. With a growing sense of "red power," coupled with a street-smart urban perspective, Indians living in cities like Milwaukee, Minneapolis and San Francisco inspired people to reclaim their Indian identity. The American Indian Movement (AIM), for example, formed in Minneapolis in 1968 to oppose a rash of police brutality upon urban Indians. Its sometimes militant tactics captured public attention, and AIM members

Ojibwe people incorporated ceremonial traditions into protest events that drew attention to flawed government policies toward American Indians. Eddie Benton (right) conducts a pipe ceremony during the Winter Dam takeover near Lac Courte Oreilles, 1971. DB

began traveling throughout Indian Country to support indigenous communities struggling against a range of injustices.[2]

Increasing numbers of attorneys were turning their attention to minority issues during this period, and tribes utilized the legal services made available through Wisconsin Judicare, a federally funded program created to assist low-income residents in the northern portion of the state.[3] The marriage of this inspired cultural movement and improved legal support fueled the *ogichidaa*—or warrior—element in upper Great Lakes Indian communities that fought for native interests. Many urban Indians renewed ties with their home reservations, where elders and traditional people gave deeper meaning to the new surge of activism. Thus began a pivotal thirty-year period as the Ojibweg battled state and local governments, special interest groups and an emerging wall of racism.

Treaty challenge on Lake Superior

Lake Superior Ojibwe fishermen stirred the legal waters in the early 1970s, bringing treaty rights to the fore in the upper Great Lakes region. Plagued by years of conflict with state officials, Ojibwe commercial fishermen sought recourse through the legal system to reaffirm their rights to fish beyond reservation boundaries. The courts examined two different treaties—1836 and 1854—and created a legal foundation for interpreting the modern-day status of the nineteenth century covenants between America and the Ojibwe nations.

The Ojibwe treaty rights movement sprouted along the south shore of Lake Superior as states worked to transform the fishery away from commercial harvest to an exclusive sportsman's preserve in the 1960s. Without regard for tribal fishing interests, Michigan and Wisconsin natural resource agencies pumped exotic salmon and trout into Gichi Gami to fill the void left by declining native lake trout populations—a result of overfishing and sea lamprey predation. At the same time, state wardens played their part by arresting tribal members and seizing their boats and nets. For Ojibwe fishermen struggling to make a living at the three centuries' old enterprise, the heavy-handed force used by state officials became unbearable.[4]

The courts were kept busy throughout 1971 as no less than three tribal fishing cases were being considered. The first stemmed from a 1965 incident when Keweenaw Bay tribal member William Jondreau was convicted in local and

Keweenaw Bay tribal fisherman Dick Semasky using a gill net to catch whitefish from Lake Superior in 1979. BE

county courts of "illegal possession of four lake trout from Keweenaw Bay," Michigan. Upon further appeal, the Michigan Supreme Court ruled that the 1854 Treaty rendered state fishing regulations for tribal members on the Bay "invalid."

Meanwhile, at the Wisconsin Supreme Court in Madison, tribal members from the Red Cliff and Bad River reservations in northern Wisconsin also opposed state jurisdiction in waters adjacent to their reservations set aside in 1854. Red Cliff's Richard Gurnoe and seven additional enrolled tribal members were arrested by conservation officers on Lake Superior for violating state game laws in the fall of 1969. During the 1971 *Gurnoe v. Wisconsin* hearing, Wisconsin Judicare attorneys representing the tribes argued that the Red Cliff and Bad River Bands retained fishing rights on Gichi Gami through the 1854 Treaty. The court agreed. While the state wielded limited police power relating to fisheries conservation and boating safety, the bands were entitled to develop their own harvest guidelines.[5]

Guns and nets became standard fishing gear for some Bay Mills fishermen in the mid-1970s. Tribal members exercising 1836 Treaty rights armed themselves after receiving gunfire from angry sportsmen at eastern Upper Michigan boat landings. BT

As the courts established these precedents along Lake Superior's south shore, Ojibwe and Ottawa bands residing farther east in the 1836 ceded territory also sought legal recourse. Eager to settle the treaty fishing status in the Great Lakes water of the eastern Upper Peninsula, the Bay Mills Indian Community and Michigan Department of Natural Resources arranged to have tribal commercial fisherman Big Abe LeBlanc cited for violating Michigan conservation laws, including fishing without a state license and use of a gill net. Initially convicted in circuit court, LeBlanc and the tribe won on appeal in 1974, and treaty bands joined leery state officials in managing the Lake Superior fishery.[6]

Wisconsin Ojibwe steer treaty journey inland

Momentum generated by the string of legal victories for Ojibwe fishing rights flowed inland in the years after 1971. Following the lead of tribes residing on Gichi Gami, Lac Courte Oreilles (LCO) Band members Fred and Mike Tribble planned for their own arrest, inspired by a classroom exercise in Ojibwe treaties taught by Larry Levanthal, an attorney and College of St. Scholastica Indian Law instructor. As members of AIM and participants of the 1971 Winter Dam takeover, the Tribbles believed in the benefits of activism. Their involvement in the three-day occupation of the Winter Dam, which created the Chippewa Flowage and flooded tribal burial grounds and the Pahquahwong community, helped draw widespread attention to the government's flawed Indian policies.[7]

In March 1974, the Tribbles notified the Wisconsin Department of Natural Resources (DNR) of their intention to spear fish through the ice on the Chippewa Flowage just beyond the LCO reservation boundary. State conservation wardens soon arrested them for possessing a fishing spear and occupying an untagged fishing shack on off-reservation waters.[8]

After the Tribbles were convicted in Sawyer County Court, the LCO Band took up the treaty rights cause by filing suit in U.S. District Court against county and state officials—including then DNR Secretary Lester Voigt—claiming unlawful interference with ceded territory hunting and fishing rights. Although the court first rejected LCO's claim in 1978, the tribe pressed on. In 1983, the U.S. Court of Appeals for the Seventh Circuit overturned the initial ruling. Known as the *Voigt* decision, three appellate judges unanimously proclaimed that the Treaties of 1837 and 1842 maintained LCO's off-reservation harvest rights for present-day tribal members whose ancestors forged the original agreements. Following the ruling, Wisconsin's five other Ojibwe tribes joined the case and the court spent the next eight years defining the nature and scope of the treaty right.[9]

With their off-reservation rights affirmed by the federal courts, Ojibwe leaders created management agencies to implement and enforce treaty harvests. Chief Buffalo descendant, Henry Buffalo Jr., played a crucial role in establishing the first such agency in 1982, the Great Lakes Indian Fisheries Commission. Ojibwe tribes residing on Lake Superior—from Grand Portage to Bay Mills—organized the fisheries commission as "a voice for tribal governments dealing with resource areas."[10]

Following the *Voigt* decision in 1983, the scope of court-protected treaty rights widened considerably. The tribes responded by forming the Voigt Intertribal Task Force to develop management and enforcement protocols for inland treaty harvests. By early 1984, tribal leaders were under growing pressure by the Bureau of Indian Affairs to streamline tribal self-regulation for both Lake Superior and the inland ceded territory. In response the tribes created the Great Lakes Indian Fish & Wildlife Commission (GLIFWC)—the marriage of the Great Lakes Indian Fisheries Commission and Voigt Intertribal Task Force. Under the leadership of Buffalo, GLIFWC was designed to provide off-reservation management for its mem-

The Voigt decision ultimately confirmed that six Ojibwe tribes retained harvest rights in the Wisconsin ceded territory: Lac Courte Oreilles, Bad River, Red Cliff, St. Croix, Lac du Flambeau, and Mole Lake.

Protesters at the Eau Pleine Reservoir. 1989. The movement opposing Ojibwe reserved rights to fish and hunt became an ugly anti-Indian campaign. GLIFWC

In 1991, a committee of federal, state and tribal managers concluded that Ojibwe fishing "has not harmed the resource" and "the fish poplulation in the [Wisconsin] ceded territory is healthy," dispelling anti-Indian claims that the tribes were destroying the fishery. Furthermore, the State Department of Tourism reported that tourism steadily increased through the late 1980s as the tribes began to exercise their rights affirmed in the Voigt *case.[14]*

Polk County sheriff deputies escort a man away from a Balsam Lake boat landing in 1990. County, state and tribal enforcement officers worked to control violent boat landing protests across northern Wisconsin. SE

ber tribes in portions of Minnesota, Wisconsin and Michigan. Like other natural resource agencies, GLIFWC was centered on resource management and conservation enforcement.[11]

Fishing in "Violence County"[12]

Off-reservation spearing under the *Voigt* decision began with a grumble in April 1985. A vocal group of non-Indian residents predicted that both the natural resources and economy of northern Wisconsin would be devastated by the treaty spearing of walleye and muskellunge in the spring and deer hunting in the autumn. The Wisconsin Department of Natural Resources publicly fueled the anti-Indian sentiment through claims that sharing the harvest and management responsibilities of the northern Wisconsin fishery with the tribes would be disastrous. Over the following years, treaty opponents mounted large demonstrations in the darkness at boat landings, oftentimes resulting in rock throwing, gunshots, death threats, and an avalanche of racial slurs, all aimed at Ojibwe spearers and their families.

From 1986 to 1990, the short jaunts Ojibwe people took from their reservation homes to ceded territory lakes rivaled the danger of any hunting trip performed by their ancestors along the old "war road." Aggressive non-Indian protesters exhibited unabashed hatred toward the Ojibweg. Crushing masses of protesters appeared night after night at the boat landings, screaming "timber nigger" and "spear a pregnant squaw, save two walleye." From the dark, forested shorelines, slingshot devices known as wrist rockets, zinged deadly ball bearings at spearers, and protest boats churned the waters, creating dangerous wakes.[13]

Local police, county sheriffs, state wardens, and GLIFWC conservation officers coordinated efforts to monitor the spearing harvest and control mobs of protesters who were often fueled by alcohol. Enforcement personnel donned riot gear, complete with helmets, hand shields, and flak jackets to face the violent crowds who pushed against the flimsy snowfencing erected around public boat launches.

While the level of protest and racism varied by year and location across the northern tier of the state, Lac du Flambeau spearers were consistently bombarded by anti-treaty elements.

A locally-based group called Stop Treaty Abuse (STA) led by restaurant owner Dean Crist tapped into the economic fears of area residents and spread misinformation about the scope and ecological impact of Ojibwe treaty harvesting. Protesters invoked a mutated sort of patriotism—that all people should be treated equally—while hurling rocks and chanting "you're a conquered nation; go home to the reservation." The focus of their energies centered on then Lac du Flambeau Tribal Judge Tom Maulson, a figurehead of Ojibwe spearing rights. Death threats rained down on Maulson along with the rocks, as he and his wife were targeted for violence.[15]

Tribal supporters rallied to counter the sensational claims made by Indian opposition groups who equated treaty fishing with environmental "rape." GLIFWC

> *Hang down your head, Tom Maulson,*
> *poor boy, you're going to die.*
> —Stop Treaty Abuse song[16]

Before the 1991 spearing season got underway, a federal lawsuit brought by Lac du Flambeau and the tribal support group, Wa-Swa-Gon Treaty Association, effectively curbed the notorious protest events at the boat landings. In *Lac du Flambeau v. Stop Treaty Abuse*, the court first issued a temporary injunction preventing STA and its members from harassing spearers at boat landings. A federal appeals court reviewing this case admonished Crist and STA and made the injunction permanent, pronouncing that "the stench of racism is unmistakable."[17]

Healing journeys

By the late 1980s, the treaty journey had become especially taxing on Wisconsin Ojibwe communities. Treaty protests had rapidly evolved into an ugly anti-Indian campaign, wearing on Ojibwe people and their supporters. GLIFWC Executive Administrator Jim Schlender saw the need for a state-wide event that offered treaty advocates a positive environment to gather and display solidarity to the public. Schlender, Wa-Swa-gon and other support groups organized "Walking Together for Peace & Justice" in June 1989, a walk/run

Cartoon by Bill Sanders in the Milwaukee Journal, 1991.

Participants of the 1990 Solidarity Run advance an American flag and staff on a tour of all the Wisconsin Ojibwe reservations, plus Lac Vieux Desert and Keweenaw Bay in Upper Michigan. AM

that traversed much of Wisconsin, from Lac du Flambeau to the state capital in Madison. Beginning with little more than a dozen participants, the southbound journey drew the support of hundreds of people by the time they walked into Madison.[18]

A river starts with only one drop of water, and while we have only a trickle here at the beginning, when we get to Madison we will have a torrent of support.
Jim Schlender, 1989
"Walking Together for
Peace & Justice"

The following month, a group of experienced runners brought together by Ernie St. Germaine embarked on the "Solidarity Run," departing from Lac du Flambeau on a tour of all the Wisconsin reservations, plus Upper Michigan's Lac Vieux Desert. Each Ojibwe community the participants visited held a reception, often including drum songs, feasting and presentations of eagle feathers that were placed on a staff the runners carried. At Mole Lake a sweat lodge ceremony was conducted. And at a stop in Red Cliff midway through the trek, a local elder blessed the runners and instructed them to put cedar in their running shoes each morning before they started.[19]

The turbulence in northern Wisconsin was felt across the United States and throughout Indian Country. Musician and native rights activist Mitch Walking Elk had followed the spearing controversy from his home in Pipestone, Minn., and by 1990 felt compelled to take action to let "the Ojibwe Nation know that they were not alone." After consulting with Tom Maulson by telephone, Walking Elk began organizing what became known as the "Peace Run" before the 1990 spring spearing season. Seeking spiritual guidance, Walking Elk offered a pipe to Steve Red Buffalo, a Lakota-Dakota from the Yankton reservation, and requested the construction of a staff that could be carried

Lac du Flambeau's Nick Hockings was named as Keeper of the Treaty Staff following the 1990 Peace Run. Hockings was charged with ensuring that specific guidelines were observed while the Staff was under his watch. The Staff was not allowed at pow wows and could not be in the presence of women during their moontime. It's use was restricted to special occasions dealing with Ojibwe treaties.[22]

from Pipestone to Lac du Flambeau.[20]

Guided by dream and prayer, Red Buffalo crafted the wooden staff in early spring, applying fur and feathers along its length. Within the staff, he placed medicines including a spirit called *wakan mani*, or walks holy. Red Buffalo completed the "Treaty Staff," as it was called, just in time for the Peace Run. Following a sweat lodge for the runners in Pipestone, the Treaty Staff was carried entirely on foot to Lac du Flambeau by Lakota, Ho Chunk, and Ojibwe, along with native people from Mexico and South America.[21]

Solidarity runners Gary Kmiecik and Fred Armell in 1990. AM

In the fall of 1990, runners in Ojibwe Country set out on a second and longer run, incorporating the Keweenaw Bay community into the spiritual relay. Over the next dozen years the run became an annual event and evolved into the "Healing Circle Run" where participants focused their prayers on health and healing for all people.[23]

Notes: Chapter Two

[1] Vine Deloria. *Custer Died for Your Sins,* 138-39; Eddie Benton interview.

[2] Lurie, 51-52; Benton interview.

[3] Lurie, 51.

[4] Cleland. *Place of the Pike,* 83; Cleland. *Rites,* 282; Sea lamprey are an exotic eel that gained access into the Great Lakes through canals constructed to accommodate the shipping industry. Biologists estimate that over the last decade, sea lamprey have become the dominant consumer of lake trout on Lake Superior, killing as much or more than commercial and sport fishermen combined.

[5] *People v. Jondreau; State v. Gurnoe.*

[6] Cleland. *The Place of the Pike,* 84, 86.

[7] Charlie Rasmussen. *Where the River is Wide,* 36-38.

[8] Satz, 94; Tribble interview.

[9] Satz, 94; Tribble.

[10] The Fond du Lac reservation, situated on the St. Louis River upstream from Lake Superior, was also a charter member of the Great Lakes Indian Fisheries Commission. *Masinaigan,* Winter 2000-01. "Some untold stories shared during Aabanaabam Conference."

[11] *Masinaigan,* Dec. 1983. "Task force state reach pact," & "Fish & wildlife commission proposed;" July 1984. "The *Voigt* Decision raises concerns."

[12] Vilas County in northeast Wisconsin earned the moniker "Violence County" among some people after years of explosive protests against Ojibwe Indians; Satz, 103.

[13] *LDF v. STA;* Kinew.

[14] *Casting Light Upon the Waters,* 13; Tim Pfaff. *Paths of the People,* 81.

[15] *LdF v. STA,* 8, 9.

[16] *LdF v. STA,* 9.

[17] *LdF v. STA,* 13 (1993).

[18] Rick Whaley. *Walleye Warriors,* 111.

[19] Kmiecik interview.

[20] Mitch Walking Elk interview. Additional "Peace Runs" followed in 1992 and 1996.

[21] Walking Elk interview. Walking Elk also carried the Treaty Staff on the Peace Run and is descended from Cheyenne, Arapaho and Hopi people.

[22] Nick Hockings interview.

[23] *Masinaigan,* "Long distance run seeks peace, spiritual healing," Fall 1990.

CHAPTER THREE:
Challenges in Minnesota

A s the tumultuous 1980s ended, the treaty journey continued into Minnesota where the western quarter of the 1837 ceded territory was parceled off by the creation of Wisconsin's state boundaries in 1848. The Mille Lacs and Fond du Lac Bands of Ojibwe Indians had watched and listened as events unfolded in Wisconsin, planning a course for treaty recognition in their east-central Minnesota homelands. Like their brethren to the east, the Minnesota bands were faced with affirming their reserved rights within the state boundary. While many Minnesota legislators exhibited a strong desire to develop an out-of-court settlement following the favorable treaty rulings in Wisconsin, opposition groups countered that citizens must fight to "save Minnesota" from the Indians.

By the time the legal dispute reached the U.S. Supreme Court in 1998, tribal members and their supporters were embracing the fusion of legal expertise and traditional Ojibwe practices. As their ancestors had done generations earlier, Ojibwe people utilized both the pipe and the pen to reach their destination.

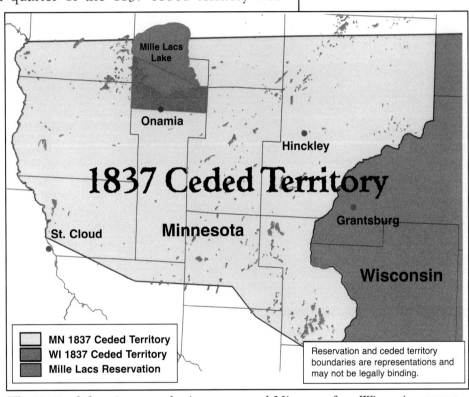

The 1837 ceded territory stretches into east-central Minnesota from Wisconsin. *SW/JG*

The trail to litigation

Following the 1983 *Voigt* decision, Mille Lacs representatives consulted with the six Wisconsin Ojibwe bands as tribal leaders planned implementation of treaty harvests. Both state and tribal negotiators recognized that as signatories to the 1837 Treaty, the Mille Lacs Band also retained treaty rights in the Wisconsin portion of the 1837 ceded territory. When modern-day spearing kicked off in the spring of 1985, Mille Lacs members fished Wisconsin lakes and in the autumn shared in the white-tailed deer harvest.[1]

While some Mille Lacs Band members traveled across the St. Croix River to harvest fish and deer in western Wisconsin, others exercised their rights closer to home, and state officials took notice. In August 1990 the Mille Lacs Band—along with a handful of its members cited for state conservation violations—filed suit in federal court against the State of Minnesota for interfering with the reserved right to hunt and fish in the 1837 ceded territory. Since the Seventh Circuit Court of Appeals had upheld the existence of treaty rights in Wisconsin, Mille Lacs appeared well-positioned in its case before the federal district court in Minnesota. Within a month, Minnesota leaders invited the Band to the bargaining table, hoping to reach a settlement and avoid a risky trial.[2]

A rash of bullet holes appeared on this Mille Lacs reservation highway sign in 1990 after the Band sought federal court recognition of their 1837 Treaty rights. *SE*

Settlement or sell-out?

Negotiators from Minnesota's Department of Natural Resources and state government spent the next two years trying to hammer out a settlement with Mille Lacs representatives. Each side made significant concessions, and by January 1993, they had come to a tentative agreement. Among the key provisions were the transfer of 7,500 acres of state land into Mille Lacs ownership, establishment of a 6,000-acre treaty fishing zone on Lake Mille Lacs, and a $10 million payment to the Band spread over five years. In exchange, Mille Lacs pledged to limit their harvest—which consisted predominately of walleye—to 24,000 pounds per year from the massive, 132,000-acre Lake Mille Lacs.[3]

As Minnesota residents and Band members mulled over the proposed settlement, the two groups splintered within their own ranks, as some felt that their leaders were selling them out to the other side. The rift appeared among Wisconsin Ojibwe tribes as well. As the Mille Lacs leadership consulted with their Wisconsin counterparts, they received differing opinions on resolving the treaty question. It was a difficult decision with consensus hard to find.[4]

There were families that were split down the middle as whether this was selling out the treaty right or whether this was a good deal. There were compromises in the settlement, but there was a lot less risk. You have to weigh all those things when you look at it.

Don Wedll, Mille Lacs Commissioner of Natural Resources, 1983-2001

Ultimately, the Wisconsin bands recognized that it was Mille Lacs' prerogative to choose the best path. Mille Lacs Chief Executive Marge Anderson called for a referendum vote to decide the issue. Tribal elders who were suspicious of a possible deal with the state government demanded assurances that there would be no tinkering with the settlement agreement after the referendum, and band members went to the polls. With a favorable response from sixty percent of the voters the measure passed, despite opposition largely centered among band members living in urban areas.[5]

Following the official approval of the Mille Lacs Assembly, the Minnesota Legislature conducted a series of hearings in late winter 1993 where state politicians listened to testimony from the differing factions and wrangled over the merits of the proposed settlement. Opponents of both the settlement and Ojibwe treaty claims, led by organizations like The Hunting And Angling Club of Minnesota, rallied around regional celebrities like retired Minnesota Vikings Football Coach Bud Grant at protests in St. Paul. The opposition groups eventually provided the driving force to quash the deal, and the settlement was voted down in the legislature.[6]

For the Mille Lacs Band there would be no more compromises with state negotiators; the referendum on the settlement agreement was intended to live or die in its original form. In June 1994, Mille Lacs presented their case against the state of Minnesota during a federal court trial in St. Paul. After three weeks of testimony and debate, Judge Diane Murphy ruled that Mille Lacs retained its right to harvest natural resources in the Minnesota 1837 ceded territory.

Throughout the mid-1990s, the 1837 Minnesota treaty case was active in the courts. A pair of judicial rulings in March 1996 affirmed that the Fond du Lac Ojibwe and the six Wisconsin bands had the same 1837 Treaty rights as Mille Lacs. In the fall of 1997, the Eighth Circuit Court of Appeals upheld the previous district court ruling that recognized off-reservation treaty rights in east-central Minnesota. Soon after the decision, band members went afield to harvest natural resources under court protection, including a white-tailed deer hunt that coincided with the Minnesota state gun opener.[8]

Although the Fond du Lac Band's 1837 Treaty case was merged with Mille Lacs', they pursued additional treaty claims in the 1854 ceded territory. In Fond du Lac v. Carlson (1996) the courts ruled that the Band also retains usufructory rights in Minnesota's Arrowhead region. The state of Minnesota, Fond du Lac Band and the tribal organization, the 1854 Authority manage natural resources in this treaty-ceded region.[7]

Former Minnesota Vikings Football Coach Bud Grant *addresses protesters on January 1993 at the Capitol in St. Paul. Grant served as the spokesman for the anti-treaty coalition Save Lake Mille Lacs Association, which opposed negotiating with the Mille Lacs Band over their reserved rights. BB*

It was during this period of courtroom activity that the Treaty Staff—as directed by spiritual leaders—was brought into the court proceedings. In St. Paul the Staff was present in the rear of the courtroom as District Judge Michael Davis heard oral arguments in October 1995. Eight months later, the Staff reappeared at a hearing before the three-judge panel of the Eighth Circuit Appellate Court. The Staff and the medicines it carried were increasingly recognized by tribal members as integral to the defense of treaty rights.

After seven years of negotiating and litigating, it seemed that the existence and scope of the 1837 Treaty right in Minnesota had been clearly decided. Well-financed opposition groups believed they could still "save Minnesota" from the Indians, however, and allied with the state in developing a legal strategy for a last-ditch appeal to the U.S. Supreme Court.

In 1995, the six Wisconsin "Voigt" tribes joined the Mille Lacs case, knowing that their 1837 reserved rights should not be limited by the arbitrary creation of a state boundary that split this treaty-ceded territory. Some recognized that an adverse ruling in the Mille Lacs case could impact off-reservation harvest rights on Wisconsin ceded lands. Yet all the bands were confident that their unity with Mille Lacs—based upon the successful exercise of treaty rights in Wisconsin—would lead to similar success in Minnesota.

The anti-treaty movement in Minnesota

After the Mille Lacs Band asserted its right to fish and hunt under the 1837 Treaty, new versions of Indian opposition groups sprang up in Minnesota under the guidance of organizations from both Wisconsin and on the national level. While their goals were similar to Wisconsin's anti-treaty organizations, the Minnesota movement made pains to avoid the racial rhetoric that became a hallmark of northern Wisconsin boatlanding protests in the late 1980s. Organizations like Proper Economic Resource Management (PERM) attempted to publicly distance themselves from the violent reputation of anti-Indian groups in Wisconsin, at times claiming benevolence toward their Ojibwe neighbors. PERM displayed well-known Minnesotans, along with a dissident tribal member, before the public to create the illusion of a broad alliance against treaty rights.

Like Protect Americans' Rights and Resources and Stop Treaty Abuse in Wisconsin, PERM incited fear in the general public through an aggressive misinformation campaign. In the words of one national researcher, these "sometimes confused, often distorted, attack[s] on tribal governments attracted legitimately distressed non-Indians as well as bigoted activists." For many white residents exposed to the hype, it appeared that Ojibwe treaty tribes were bent on wrongfully usurping all the land and resources within the Minnesota 1837 ceded territory.[9]

In an effort to make tribal harvesting rights seem menacing and environmentally destructive, opposition groups routinely lumped unrelated Indian issues into their messages to the public. Conspiracies involving casinos, reservation boundaries, land trust initiatives and tribal jurisdiction were woven into their publications and speeches to arouse suspicion. State Senator Steve Morse noted at a 1993 settlement hearing that "every issue dealing with Indians is being brought up. We don't like to use the word racism, but I think that's what it is. This has to do with a contractual agreement that our country entered into with the band of Chippewa."[10]

Another approach of the anti-treaty forces centered on portraying Indians as victims of their trust relationship with the U.S. government. These groups argued that the remaining tribal sovereignty and fragments of tribal homelands should be taken away so that the Ojibwe could be integrated into mainstream America. The concepts of assimilation and termination that formed the cornerstones of brash mid-twentieth century federal policies were resurrected and billed as the antidote for a people plagued—not only by federal recognition of tribal governments—but by their own culture.[11]

Legal bills mounted through the 1990s for the landowners who joined the suit against the tribe as the courts consistently upheld the Ojibweg reserved rights, and PERM banquets became increasingly important to pay attorney's fees. Adopting the role as "fundraising arm for the Landowners," PERM collected more than 1.25 million dollars. Styled after dinners sponsored by conservation organizations, PERM volunteers raffled hunting guns and auctioned wildlife prints. Speakers took the podium to motivate the PERM membership with battlefield and fourth-quarter football analogies, and sponsors like *Minnesota Outdoor News* were recognized for their financial and editorial support. Banquets also provided a forum where a disgruntled tribal member could tell a homogeneous white audience about the ills of reservation politics, thus marginally supporting PERM claims of being a non-racial, cross-cultural movement.[12]

At a February 1998 PERM banquet in Blaine, Minnesota an attorney representing Mille Lacs area landowners reported that the state and his clients would petition the U.S. Supreme Court to hear issues regarding *Mille Lacs v. Minnesota*. Citing recent judicial rulings against tribal claims in other regions of the U.S., the landowners' attorney predicted victory, should the high court accept the appeal. The appeal centered on three issues: President Taylor's 1850 Removal Order, Mille Lacs' 1855 Treaty,

A GLIFWC enforcement officer conducts a field check near Mille Lacs in November 1997. Tribal members hunted off-reservation following a ruling from the Eight Circuit Court of Appeals that upheld reserved harvest rights. COR

National anti-Indian groups and the Wisconsin-based PARR helped organize tribal opponents in Minnesota. Violent protests never materialized in Minnesota, and groups like PERM focused on fundraising and a media campaign against the tribes. SE

and the impact of Minnesota's statehood on treaty rights. State attorneys alleged that each one of these events terminated the band's 1837 Treaty rights.

Despite the unanimous findings of federal court judges over the past five years, the Supreme Court opted to have a closer look at the *Mille Lacs v. Minnesota* case. The parties were notified to submit their written briefs before oral arguments scheduled for December 1998. Nine justices from the highest court in the country would issue the final ruling on rights reserved by Ojibwe chiefs in 1837.

Treaty fishermen spearing walleye on Lake Mille Lacs in April 1998. Tribal members exercised off-reservation rights in Minnesota 1837 ceded territory as the U.S. Supreme Court considered an appeal by the State. COR

The shaking tent

After the U.S. Supreme Court announced its decision to hear the appeal filed by treaty opponents, tribal leaders began mobilizing for the journey to Washington DC. Many people in Ojibwe communities were initially stunned by the high court's decision; the existence and scope of 1837 Treaty rights had been affirmed in two states by several federal courts without disagreement. Moreover, the Supreme Court itself had previously refused to review the *Voigt* decision 15 years earlier.

In July 1998, the GLIFWC Board of Commissioners gathered in Lac du Flambeau for a routine bimonthly meeting. Tribal leaders used this occasion to voice their concerns about the forthcoming Supreme Court hearing in December when an echo from the recent past entered the conversation: should the Ojibwe seek a negotiated settlement with the state of Minnesota? After all, would the highest court in the nation now accept this case to simply agree with the lower courts? The answer was unsettling. In recent years the Supreme Court reversed lower courts' rulings 93% of the time in cases dealing with states' rights issues.[13]

Meanwhile, a contingent of Ojibwe officials and spiritual leaders from Ontario were meeting with other GLIFWC staff nearby in preparation for a

Commission-sponsored binational Treaty Conference, an historic gathering that would bring Ojibwe people from the U.S. and Canada together on Madeline Island in September. In need of spiritual guidance, the GLIFWC Commissioners had earlier requested that the Canadians conduct a *jiisakaan*, or shaking tent—a ceremony that seeks advice from the spirits—during their visit.

That July evening people gathered at *Waswagoning* (torch lake), a nineteeth century Ojibwe village replica located at Lac du Flambeau. Operated by Nick Hockings, Waswagoning serves as an educational center and a gathering place where traditional Ojibwe practices are embraced. Near sundown under clear skies a handful of Indian people from the Ojibways of Onigaming community in Ontario constructed the shaking tent—a narrow, tubular structure made sturdy with cedar poles and planed wood covered with blankets. A question prepared by Ojibwe leaders was posed during the three-hour ceremony conducted entirely in *Ojibwemowin:* should they pursue negotiations with the state or allow the Supreme Court to decide?[14]

Just before midnight, Onigaming Ojibway Fred Kelly addressed those seated on the grass around the tent, translating the spirit's spoken word into English: compromise is not an option. Ojibwe leaders are to proceed united and avoid individual dealings with the opposition. Any separate negotiations with the state would side-track everyone and compromise treaty rights held by all. Furthermore, Kelly related that the Treaty Staff should be taken to the Supreme Court, and tribal attorneys were to put cedar in their shoes before the hearing.[15]

As the end of summer 1998 drew near, native people across the nation looked ahead to the Court hearing and its potential ramifications across Indian Country. For the average tribal member—as well as the Ojibwe leadership—little else could be done to assist in legal preparations for the late autumn hearing. That part of the journey was in the hands of the attorneys. The spiritual path—one paved by creation stories, cosmology and tradition—however, welcomed many travelers in the coming months on a return trip to Washington DC.

Ojibwe representatives from GLIFWC and the Canada-based Kabapikotawangag Resources Council met on Madeline Island in September 1998 to sign the Anishinaabe Aki Protocol. Growing tribal solidarity across the international border fostered exchanges in cultural traditions and natural resource management techniques. COR

Waswagoning at Lac du Flambeau provided a traditional setting where people gathered for a shaking tent ceremony as tribal leaders deliberated over the forthcoming U.S. Supreme Court hearing. SE

Notes: Chapter Three

[1] The fish and game taken by Mille Lacs Band members were included in harvest quotas established by the St. Croix Tribe.

[2] Roger and Priscilla Buffalohead. *Against the Tide of American History,* 112; Wedll interview.

[3] *Mille Lacs Messenger,* "DNR and Band unveil the details,"; *New Ulm Journal,* "DNR, Mille Lacs officials outline pact;" Wedll interview.

[4] *M.L.M.,* "Messenger Mailbag: No one should sell their rights;" *M.L.M.,* "Nothing is certain about Band's vote;" Wedll interview.

[5] *M.L.M.,* "Mille Lacs Band gives thumbs up to settlement;" Wedll interview.

[6] *M.L.M,* "Heated words exchanged at the Capitol rally;" *New Ulm Journal,* "DNR, Mille Lacs officials outline pact;" Wedll interview.

[7] The 1854 Authority is a natural resource management agency representing two Ojibwe bands that have reserved rights in northeast Minnesota: Bois Forte and Grand Portage.

[8] *Masinaigan,* "First Treaty Harvest Underway in Minnesota 1837 ceded territory."

[9] *Outdoor News* [MN], "Capitol rally sends message;" Rudolf C. Ryser, "Anti-Indian movement on the Tribal Frontier."

[10] *Hibbing Daily Tribune,* "Mille Lacs settlement backer charges racism in some critics."

[11] PERM newsletter, Position Paper.

[12] *Outdoor News* [MN], Jan. 11, 2002: "Outdoor Insights," 3; O.N., Jan. 18, 2002: "DNR says no observers at state-tribal meeting," p. 14; PERM newsletter, Jan. 2000; Wedll interview.

[13] *Mille Lacs v. Minn.,* Declaration of David Getches; Rasmussen, Journal, July 28, 1998.

[14] Rasmussen Journal.

[15] Ibid.

CHAPTER FOUR:
The Waabanong Run

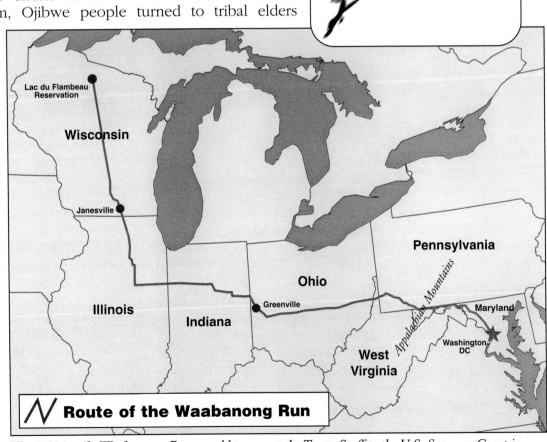

The reaffirmation of treaty rights in the late twentieth century helped to spur a cultural renaissance across Ojibwe communities in the upper Great Lakes region. For many, the return to the ceded territory lakes and woodlands cherished by their ancestors was accompanied by a growing self-awareness of a common past. After 150 years of efforts to force their acculturation into the American mainstream, Ojibwe people turned to tribal elders to reclaim their Indian identities. Tapping the wisdom of grandmothers and grandfathers, tribal members who had a marginal understanding of the past embraced traditional skills, Ojibwe-mowin and teachings of the *Midewiwin*—the traditional religion before the influence of Christian missionaries.

Just as individuals experienced a heightened perception of Ojibwe traditions, tribal governments and other Indian organizations followed suit. Among them, the Great Lakes Indian Fish & Wildlife Commission (GLIFWC) pledged "to infuse traditional Anishinaabe culture and values" into the agency's approach to

Route of the Waabanong Run

The 1,000-mile Waabanong Run would transport the Treaty Staff to the U.S. Supreme Court in Washington DC entirely on foot. SW (Inset) This logo created by Francis Kmiecik appeared on Waabanong Run support vehicles.

43

Runners received eagle feathers and were taught a pipe loading song for the journey to Washington DC. COR

natural resource management and environmental protection. Guided by Ojibwe spiritual leader Eddie Benton, this commitment was incorporated into the GLIFWC Mission Statement following the 1992 Strategic Planning Conference at Keweenaw Bay. With treaty rights now on trial at the U.S. Supreme Court, members of the Commission reflected upon this cultural directive and sought the aid of powers beyond legal expertise.

A good way

By early autumn of 1998, attorneys representing Mille Lacs and seven other bands had completed legal briefs destined for the Supreme Court. Marking the accomplishment, GLIFWC hosted a traditional feast on September 24 in Odanah where Red Cliff's Mike Montano conducted a pipe ceremony and smudged each brief with sage. The documents outlined tribal positions on the three major points under consideration by the court: the 1850 Removal Order, the 1855 Treaty, and the impact of Minnesota's statehood on treaty rights.[1]

As participants in the spiritual runs and walks that occurred in 1989-1990, GLIFWC's Neil Kmiecik and Jim Schlender recognized an opportunity to tap into the hopes, prayers, and good thoughts of treaty supporters with an event. Kmiecik, a veteran runner and head of the Commission's Biological Services Division, suggested carrying the Treaty Staff on a cross-country run—from northern Wisconsin to Washington DC. Based on Kmiecik's past experiences and instruction from spiritual people, delivering the staff to the Supreme Court on foot seemed to be "a good way" to fulfill the jiisakaan directive.

Following a round of telephone calls to tribes across Ojibwe Country in October, Schlender and Kmiecik recruited a pair of elders from the St. Croix area—Gene and Eva Connor—to commit to the 1000-mile journey. Tribes were asked to spon-

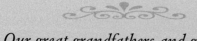

Our great grandfathers and grandmothers walked where you will run. Tobacco will go out every day and we will follow you every day as you run to Washington DC.

Marge Anderson
November 10, 1998

44

sor a runner from their membership; however, the short notice made enlisting people challenging.

Cash donations soon trickled in and so did runners, answering the call of the michitweg. Most GLIFWC-member tribes provided financial support, as did the Leech Lake and Bois Forte Ojibwe. The largest contribution came from the Grand Traverse Band, an 1836 Treaty tribe from the northeast corner of Lower Michigan active in exercising their reserved rights on the Great Lakes. Schlender soon learned that Mille Lacs and his home reservation, Lac Courte Oreilles, were sending runners to join him, Kmiecik and the Connors. The group now totaled eleven and formed the core of the Waabanong Run—the journey "back to the East."[2]

Ojibwe elders and leaders carry the Treaty Staff along Lac du Flambeau's *Bear River. SE*

On the eve of the run, participants and supporters braved gusting winds in excess of 50 miles-per-hour to attend a feast and ceremony at Lac du Flambeau. Elders from throughout Great Lakes Ojibwe Country were on hand with words of prayer and encouragement for the michitweg as they readied to meet the challenges of the run. Tobasonakwut Kinew, from the Ojibways of Onigaming community in Ontario, taught the runners a pipe-loading song to be used in ceremonies along the way. In addition, the michitweg received a cluster of colored ribbons that included an eagle feather to pin on their left shoulder as they ran.[3]

A sweat lodge ceremony scheduled that evening was postponed due to the severe weather conditions. The ice and wind storm toppled trees and brought down power lines across the region, sending utility workers and the Minocqua Fire Department scrambling to mend the damage. It seemed an ominous precursor to the long run ahead. Some tribal

The Waabanong Run's core team—those committed to the entire 17-day journey—were comprised of both walkers and runners, collectively referred to as runners or michitweg, meaning those who carry the words, in Ojibwemowin. Supplemental runners joined in to carry the staffs throughout the journey as well.[6]

observers, however, were heartened by the powerful display—the spirits from the west were gathering at Lac du Flambeau.[4]

The southern route

The runners awoke to frigid west winds that had gusted throughout the night. A blanket of snow spread across the northern landscape, and ice glistened on the billowing trees. Soon after sunrise, the michitweg and their supporters gathered around a ceremonial fire under the towering red pines at Lac du Flambeau's Bear River Pow Wow grounds.

Core runners Bo Hammond, Don Graves and Erik Gahbow in northern Wisconsin. SE

As a bald eagle watched from its nearby roost, asemaa-filled pipes circulated through the mass that huddled around the fire. Additional asemaa was passed for people to hold and pray with before sprinkling into the fire. The roaring winds lifted the burning tobacco smoke skyward, symbolic of prayers rising to the Creator. Tobasonakwut Kinew called for the michitweg to circle around the fire and smudged each one with a large eagle feather and a shell containing burning sage. The Treaty Staff and two other staffs that runners would carry were also smudged and the michitweg were reminded to put cedar in their shoes. Despite the bone-chilling weather, Kinew did not rush the ceremony, and people were patient; everyone involved wanted the journey to begin in a good way.

The Waabanong Run began with a brief walk as tribal leaders and elders carried the Treaty Staff through the cathedral of pines along the Bear River and out to the entrance of the pow wow grounds. There runners from Lac Courte Oreilles and Mille Lacs received the Staff and began running with the west wind swirling all around them.

While most of Waabanong's core team had some running experience, few had very much. The three michitweg from Mille Lacs—Donald Graves, Joel Shaugobay and Erik Gahbow—were recent converts to regular jogging as they

46

worked to get in better physical condition. In fact, Graves and Shaugobay had less than a month of training behind them before committing to the Run.[5]

Some of the stronger runners like Gahbow and Lac Courte Oreilles' Bo Hammond and George "Budman" Morrow were eager to advance the Staff down the road and ran up to five-mile stretches that first day. Other runners, including Larry and Randy Miller, brothers from LCO, performed better under shorter stretches. To avoid confusion, distances for the core team were standardized to one mile, and a daily rotation was drawn up that established a running order.

With limited funding, the core team took lodging in a variety of locations—with friends, supporters and in Indian communities along the way. On the first evening, they booked rooms at a Merrill, Wisconsin motel after covering 66 miles. Day 1 ended as it began—in ceremony. Before their evening meal, the runners gathered in a hotel room for a pipe ceremony and talking circle, an opportunity to reflect on the day's journey, express gratitude to the Creator, and oftentimes, to acknowledge those families left at home.

Before sunrise the following morning, the michitweg were smudged in an empty corner of the motel parking lot. During the ceremony, they were asked to include Supreme Court Justice Anthony Kennedy in their prayers as they ran.

This practice of praying for particular individuals was rooted in Kmiecik's experience on the 1990 Big Foot Memorial Ride from Bridger to Wounded Knee, South Dakota. Kmiecik, a Lakota from Standing Rock, and others ran alongside riders on horseback on a 5-day trek that traced the route taken by Big Foot's Minneconjou and some of Sitting Bull's Hunkpapa people in December 1890; after arriving at Wounded Knee on the Pine Ridge reservation, approximately 300 of their number—women, children and men—were massacred by the U.S. 7th Calvary. A century later, participants on the Memorial Ride prayed for a "specific part of the nation" each day.[7]

With Justice Kennedy in mind, the Waabanong runners continued south on roads that paralleled U.S. Highway 51. A mix of ice and snow frozen to the shoulder of the roads created hazardous footing conditions. South of Stevens Point, the forest increasingly gave way to agriculture as they neared the ceded

Veteran runner Neil Kmiecik helped organize the Run with direction from spiritual leaders and his own experience. *JS*

North of Madison, the michitweg found themselves traveling the same route that conservationist and "forest reserve" advocate John Muir used more than 130 years earlier while attending the University of Wisconsin. The wooded preserves Muir championed evolved into National Forests on ceded lands in Wisconsin and Michigan where Ojibwe Indians continue to hunt, fish and harvest wild plants.[9]

Runners placed sprigs of cedar in their shoes each morning. *JS*

The michitweg relayed the staffs at one-mile intervals for more than one thousand miles. Supplemental runners joined the relay rotation throughout the journey and occasionally covered longer stretches of road. *COR*

territory's southern boundary. That evening they backtracked several miles and stayed at the home of Jean Day, Ho-Chunk, who provided food, traditional medicine and tobacco ties. She saw the runners off the next morning, telling them "each step is a prayer."

The wintry temperatures rebounded, rising into the middle forties. Justice Sandra Day O'Connor occupied many prayers, and a host of supplemental runners joined the core team on Day 3. The day was marked by loss, however, when Don Graves learned that his mother-in-law had walked on to the spirit world, hastening his return to Minnesota to support his family. An eagle feather was also lost somewhere in central Wisconsin, one of four attached to the smallest of the three staffs.[8]

Bodies aching and minor injuries swelling, the group of michitweg found their way south of Madison the following day. Kmiecik's two sons and a brother—all accomplished runners—provided a welcome boost to the core team, on some occasions covering five-mile stretches. Meanwhile, the one-mile-relay structure suited the core team well, allowing them frequent opportunities to rest throughout the day. Schlender, Gene Connor and the walkers who joined them often leap-frogged ahead of the running rotation, using roadside markers to delineate the miles they covered.

Bad River Band member and public television news anchor Patty Loew and her husband David Braga hosted the Waabanong runners at their rural Madison home that evening. Tucked away on the wooded Loew-Braga property, a sweat lodge, reconstructed by Potowatami firekeeper Art Shegonee, was readied for the michitweg. Tobasonakwut Kinew arrived and conducted the sweat lodge ceremony where he advised the runners that the lost eagle feather should be "let go" and not replaced. A feast immediately followed the evening ceremony, including spaghetti, apple crisp, cookies and fresh bread, and local doctor Peter Hanson was on hand, volunteering his time to evaluate running-related ailments.

The spiritual fortification some runners experienced at the sweat lodge was amplified the next morning at the Heider farm in Janesville where the white buffalo calf Miracle was born in August 1994. Now a young adult with a calf of her own, Miracle's coat had changed from white to shades of black, red and yellow—just as native oral traditions had prophesized. After consulting with owner Dave Heider, the runners gathered on the edge of Miracle's fenced pasture that had been adorned with thousands of mementos and began a pipe ceremony. The great buffalo casually approached the circled group of runners as the pipe was loaded and remained there watching, little more than an arm's length away, until the ceremony was complete. Miracle then retreated back into the pasture. All those present recognized something special had happened.[10]

Before leaving the farm, Heider presented the runners with an offering bundled in a tiny pouch and tied it to the Treaty Staff. By early afternoon, the Run had progressed across the Illinois border and the michitweg took lodging in Belvidere.

Over the next two days, the runners continued south along gravel backroads and narrow state highways, maintaining a generous buffer from the heavy traffic of the Chicago metropolitan area. The countryside was dominated by intensively-managed agricultural fields; there were few fence rows and only a hint of gravel shoulders skirting the highways. Otherwise, the plow, scattered farm houses and sprawling subdivisions claimed the land.

Miracle and her calf Millennium in Janesville, Wis. 1998. COR

Heading east—Waabanong

After a full week on the Waabanong Run, the minds and bodies of the core team grew in strength. With a staff in hand, individuals had covered anywhere from 35 to 50 miles. The days began and ended in ceremonies that included asemaa, sage and Ojibwemowin. Runners were developing a greater appreciation of Ojibwe cosmology and how they fit into that world.[11]

Approximately 70 miles southwest of Chicago, the course of the run turned due east. Even though the michitweg were far from their northwoods homes, daily encounters with birds and animals reinforced their feeling of affinity with the natural world. Through much of Wisconsin, eagles were regularly spotted and later, hawks circled the skies above. Eva Connor seemed to attract the most

White-tailed deer, bald eagles and hawks made *frequent appearances, providing a sense of well being for many runners.* COR

attention from the animal nations, especially near farms where dogs and horses often bolted to the roadsides, running alongside her.[12]

The St. Croix elder also drew the admiration and respect of the runners, most of whom were less than half her age. Connor's strength and running endurance inspired the young michitweg to overcome the physical and mental hurdles that they encountered. Husband Gene Connor's zeal for walking and infectious smile further lifted the spirits of the entire group.[13]

At a sunrise ceremony in Remington, Indiana, Justice Clarence Thomas became the eighth member of the high court included in the runner's prayers. On that ninth day, the Run stretched eastward 90 miles—around 25 miles longer than daily averages—with the support of a half-dozen extras that included GLIFWC volunteers, Ball State University Professor Larry Nesper and a number of Ball State students. The reappearance of woodlots, hills and continued mild temperatures hovering in the 50s made for enjoyable running. In fact, except for the powerful storm that launched the Run in northern Wisconsin, the michitweg were blessed with ideal weather on their eastward journey. That evening the Miami Indians welcomed the michitweg to their tribal center in Peru, Indiana where a pipe ceremony and talking circle rounded out an exceptional day.

Before dawn the following morning, the smells of biscuits and gravy greeted the core team as they awoke on army-style cots at the Miami Tribal Center. The tribal genealogist served up breakfast, and the michitweg conducted a smudging ceremony where runners were reminded to keep the final Supreme Court Justice, David Souter, in their prayers. Back on the road, they made good time as they penetrated western Ohio. Near sundown, they came into Greenville and stopped at a monument where the United States and a number of tribal nations, including the Ojibwe,

Food, energy drinks, sleeping bags and spare clothes accompanied the michitweg *from Mille Lacs and Lac Courte Oreilles in this passenger van.* COR

Miami, Kickapoo, Kaskaskia, Ottawa, Potawatomi, and Delaware, negotiated the 1795 Treaty that established a number of U.S.-tribal boundaries in the Midwest.[14]

Mille Lacs' Don Graves returned to the group that evening after attending funeral services for his mother-in-law in Minnesota. Graves spoke fondly of his wife, Kathy, and the sacrifice she made: "Her loss was very deep, but she encouraged me to go back. My wife knew how important this [Run] was to me, the Mille Lacs Band, and to other American Indians."[15]

On Graves' first day back, he logged eight hard-running miles. Runners and walkers tallied 80 miles on the day, and local ranch owner Barbara Crandall guided the group to her property for an evening feast. Largely isolated from her Indian heritage, Crandall embraced the opportunity to support the runners and participate in ceremonies.

The mountains arrive

Near Columbus, Ohio on the 12th day, the michitweg encountered long uphill stretches of road shadowed by hardwoods. Several AIM members and supporters from Cincinnati who had heard about the Run offered to relay a staff through the busy Columbus metro area. With eagle feathers pinned on their shoulders, these veteran runners covered 22 miles of sometimes difficult urban terrain and met the core team east of the city where the two groups smoked a pipe and said goodbye.

Eva Connor is trailed by Erik Gahbow and Budman Morrow in Maryland. Runners were tested by long inclines and steep hills through the mountainous eastern states. SE

Across the northern arm of West Virginia and into Pennsylvania, the broad, rolling hills continued eastward, leading the runners high into the Allegheny and Appalachian Mountains. In southwest Pennsylvania another supporter with Indian heritage (Lenni Lenape), Delores Jones, provided food and lodging at a hunting cabin situated 2,500 feet up the western edge of the Alleghenies. The michitweg welcomed Jones' family and friends in their customary pipe ceremony and talking circle before feasting on turkey, potatoes, dressing and salad.

Having traversed more than 800 miles across the United States, the core team—all residents of the western Lake Superior region—took note of the difficulties that native people face in the east. On November 25, the runner's daily journal remarked that "many of the Indian people we have met aren't part of a recognized tribe and are struggling to maintain a connection with their Indian identity." The observation reinforced the importance of seeking out the wisdom of elders and protecting tribal homelands. Without such diligence, it seemed, bands residing to the west may share the same fate as those in the east.[16]

Beginning at Uniontown, Pennsylvania, the mountains sprouted one after another. Both runners and walkers were tested, taking turns on the steep inclines that measured up to 3.5 miles. It took several days and many hard miles to reach the eastern face of the mountains. During that time the michitweg prayed for women, "the strength" of Indian nations, and those people plagued by sickness and addiction.[17]

Thirty miles northwest of Washington DC, the Waabanong Run reached Frederick, Maryland on the eve of Thanksgiving. The michitweg would spend the next two nights at the Quaker Meeting House. The Quakers and Waabanong team shared several meals together, including a Thanksgiving potluck dinner. Both groups took time to conduct their ceremonies, as each respectfully looked on.[18]

On Day 17, the michitweg were poised to complete the run. After holding what would be the final talking circle, Eva Connor, Budman Morrow and Erik Gahbow ran the first mile, each holding one of the three staffs. After several rotations in the relay order, the runners soon entered Georgetown on the edge of Washington DC. With the Treaty Staff in hand, Gahbow entered the city where a beehive of cars, trucks and people seemed to

Michitweg assemble on the steps of the Supreme Court after their 17-day journey. SE

envelop him. Riding in support vehicles, the Waabanong group combed the busy streets looking for him, but were resigned to park and wait at the Supreme Court. While the michitweg assembled, Kmiecik set out on foot, spotting Gahbow less than a mile away. The two core runners then brought the Treaty Staff onto the steps of the Supreme Court where the michitweg cheered their arrival.

The gathering in Washington DC

While most of the core runners planned on remaining in Washington through the court hearing, a handful had commitments at home and returned—

this time seated in cars and on passenger jets. A great movement of tribal supporters, however, was just making its way to the nation's capital.

Located among the row houses a few blocks from the Supreme Court, the National Indian Gaming Association (NIGA) offered its building as a gathering place. In the fenced backyard, Red Cliff's Leo and Richard LaFernier built a fire on November 28 where people socialized and conducted ceremonies over the next four days. The Waabanong michitweg, attorneys, tribal leaders and treaty supporters filtered through the yard, sitting by the sacred fire, and eating wild rice and venison dishes from a basement kitchen tended by Sokaogon *ogichidaakwe*, Fran Van Zile.

As dawn broke over the eastern seaboard on December 2, a great host of people circled the sacred fire. Elders and tribal leaders were seated on chairs close to the fire; many stood and spoke during the lengthy sunrise ceremony. The three staffs from the Waabanong Run were smudged with sage, Mille Lacs' Little Otter Drum group sang and attorneys Marc Slonim and Howard Bichler were reminded to put cedar in their shoes. The ceremony concluded with a Midewiwin song by St. Croix's Lewis Taylor.

Under a police escort, the treaty supporters formed a deep procession in the street before the NIGA building, walking the short distance to the massive courthouse after the ceremony. The Little Otter Drum started up again, this time before the highest court in the United States. Sokaogon judge and long-

GLIFWC's Jim Schlender holds a pipe at the sunrise ceremony held near the Supreme Court on December 2. Tribal representatives from the upper Great Lakes region and elsewhere traveled to Washington to support Mille Lacs. COR

Waabanong runners in denim ribbon shirts escort the Treaty Staff to the Supreme Court building prior to the start of the Minnesota v. Mille Lacs *hearing.* COR

time treaty advocate Fred Ackley joined in with a whistle crafted from an eagle wing bone. While supporters danced and sang, the michitweg grouped around the Treaty Staff, maneuvering through the mass of onlookers and up the broad series of steps leading to the entrance. Before the final landing of the great staircase, the runners broke rank. Kmiecik and Gahbow took the Treaty Staff to a side entrance where a Waabanong mitchiwe performed a brief ceremony, adding water to the tiny bundle white buffalo owner Dave Heider had presented to the runners several weeks earlier. By previous arrangement, the Supreme Court Clerk then graciously allowed them access to his office near the courtroom where a speaker broadcasted the proceedings. In accordance with Supreme Court policy, the Staff could not be in the courtroom during the hearing. With some difficulty, the remaining runners managed to gain seating assignments in the capacity-filled courtroom. The final act of the Waabanong Run was realized—the staff had been delivered.

Mille Lacs' Attorney Marc Slonim addresses reporters following the Supreme Court hearing. COR

Minnesota v. Mille Lacs[19]

After people settled into the high-backed pews of the cavernous hall of justice, a buzzer sounded, the Court was pronounced in session and the justices emerged single file from a seam in the burgundy drapes that hung behind the bench. The audience rose to their feet and remained standing until the nine members of the high court were seated.

During the hour-long hearing that followed, two attorneys from each side split the time fielding questions from the court. Often interrupted by the justices as they spoke, the four lawyers were grilled on three issues: whether Mille Lacs relinquished its treaty rights by signing an 1855 Treaty, if Minnesota's statehood designation eliminated treaty rights, and the legality of the 1850 Executive Order—that disastrous attempt to remove Wisconsin and Michigan Ojibwe bands west of the Mississippi. The court spared neither legal team from rigorous scrutiny.

Much of the tough questioning centered on the nature of President Taylor's Executive Order that called for removal to unceded lands and purported to revoke the property rights reserved by the Ojibweg. Although a lower federal court had deemed Taylor's order "unlawful," some Supreme Court justices sought to determine if the revocation element of the order could be enforced separately. Mille Lacs Attorney Marc Slonim argued that since revocation was intended as a tool for removal and removal plans had been abandoned, the 1837 Treaty right was still intact—the two parts of the order were inseverable. United States Attorney Barbara McDowell followed Slonim in support of Mille Lacs and fielded a volley of inquiries from the justices.[20]

Treaty Rights and Statehood: Lessons from Wisconsin

Did Minnesota's statehood terminate 1837 Treaty rights? That was one key question considered by the Supreme Court. Minnesota officials asserted that statehood did indeed terminate off-reservation rights, and moreover, that treaty rights are incompatible with their sovereign responsibility to manage natural resources.

In a brief submitted to the Court, Wisconsin bands dispelled that argument by recounting the 15-year success of cooperative tribal-state resource management under the Voigt case. The bands informed the Supreme Court of "cutting edge" fishery monitoring and assessment work conducted by state and GLIFWC biologists that has benefited everyone. Furthermore, the bands noted, the court in the Voigt case praised the cooperative management system: "Both the tribes and the officials of the State of Wisconsin responsible for implementing the tribes' treaty rights can take pride in their accomplishment. They deserve widespread recognition and appreciation for their efforts."[21] Ultimately, the bands demonstrated that treaty rights are an accepted part of life in Wisconsin and have yielded many positive benefits.

The "Wisconsin story" of treaty rights implementation apparently caught the eye of Supreme Court Justice Sandra Day O'Connor. She appeared skeptical of Minnesota's claim that its sovereignty would be unacceptably infringed upon when—in her initial line of questions—she probed Minnesota Assistant Attorney General John Kirwin about "what has been worked out in Wisconsin."[22]

The lively and sometimes enigmatic hearing ended without any clear indication of how the justices might rule. The michitweg and treaty supporters returned to the NIGA building to share one last meal and ceremony before leaving for their homes. The high court would remain silent for almost four months before issuing its benchmark ruling on Ojibwe treaty rights.

Notes: Chapter Four

[1] *Masinaigan,* Winter 98-99. "Treaty rights on trial once again."

[2] GLIFWC, Waabanong Run financial report.

[3] *Lakeland Times,* Nov. 13, 1998. "High winds topple trees and power lines," 1, 12.

[4] *Masinaigan Supplement,* "The Waabanong Run from Wisconsin to DC;" *Lakeland Times.*

[5] Waabanong Runners from Mille Lacs interview by author, March 9, 1999.

[6] For more on the word michitwe see *A Dictionary of the Ojibway Language* by Frederic Baraga.

[7] *The Rapid City Journal.* Dec. 29, 1990, "Big Foot Ride fulfills dream." p. A1; Kmeicik interview.

[8] This staff kept by Neil Kmeicik had been a gift from Jean Day.

[9] Stephen Fox. *The American Conservation Movement.* pp. 37, 109-110.

[10] *News from Indian Country,* Late Feb. 2000, "She was born white, and they named her Miracle," 10-11B.

[11] Mille Lacs interview.

[12] Ibid.

[13] Mille Lacs interview; Waabanong Runners from Lac Courte Oreillles interview.

[14] GLIFWC, "Treaty Rights," p. 33; See Ronald Satz, *Classroom Activities in Wisconsin Indian Treaties and Tribal Sovereignty* (Madison, 1996) for more on the struggle of various groups to achieve recognition.

[15] Mille Lacs interview.

[16] Sketch, 11; Mille Lacs interview.

[17] Sketch, 12.

[18] *Frederick News-Post,* "Tribe on thousand mile quest," 1.

[19] Originally know as *Mille Lacs v. Minnesota,* the case title was inverted to identify the state as the petitioner.

[20] *Mille Lacs v. Minn.,* 861 F. Supp. 784, (D.Minn 1994), 785; *Minnesota v. Mille Lacs,* 97-1337. Supreme Court of the United States, Official Transcript, 36.

[21] Brief by Bad River and LdF 1997, 12.

[22] *Minnesota v. Mille Lacs,* Supreme Court transcript, 7; *Minnesota v. Mille Lacs,* Brief, 12.

CHAPTER FIVE:
The Spirits at Sandy Lake

The final years of the twentieth century witnessed closure and continuity in the Ojibwe journey. Major problems in the history of Lake Superior area Ojibwe people, including Minnesota 1837 Treaty rights and the Sandy Lake legacy, were addressed in a few short years. And the continued growth of cultural foundations rooted in Ojibwemowin, traditional lifeways and ceremony made clear that the present generation had plotted a course that would help guide the Ojibwe journey far into the future.

The highest law in the land

After the vigorous round of questioning conducted by many Supreme Court justices during the *Minnesota v. Mille Lacs* hearing, few observers publicly predicted how the court would rule. Mille Lacs Chief Executive Marge Anderson sought to prepare the band for both favorable and unfavorable decisions. In either scenario, Anderson called for unity between all who revered Lake Mille Lacs: "When this historic decision comes down, it must mark the end of bitterness and disharmony."[1]

On March 24, 1999 the Supreme Court published its decision, concluding that Ojibwe treaty claims in the 1837 Minnesota ceded territory were indeed valid and not terminated by any subsequent acts of federal or state government. Justice Sandra Day O'Connor drafted the majority opinion of the Court in the 5-4 ruling, explaining that the law and the evidence supported the continued existence of 1837 Treaty rights to hunt, fish and gather.

The Court found that Mille Lacs did not relinquish its reserved rights when it entered into the 1855 Treaty, nor did the tribe lose its rights when Minnesota was admitted into the Union. As for the Removal Order, which received considerable attention at the hearing nearly four months earlier, O'Connor wrote that because the plaintiffs "have pointed to no colorable source of authority for the President's removal order, we agree

The Ojibweg journey home *following the infamous Sandy Lake annuity payment was the subject of a 2002 GLIFWC poster.* COR

Bad River tribal members fish Lake Mille Lacs.
The Supreme Court issued their ruling upholding reserved rights in time for the spring harvest season. COR

with the Court of Appeals' conclusion that the 1850 removal order was unauthorized." Neither the 1837 Treaty nor Congress gave President Taylor the power to remove the Ojibwe. Moreover, since the removal part of the order was invalid, so too was the portion purporting to revoke "usufructory privileges." As Mille Lacs attorney Marc Slonim had argued, the two parts of the order were inseverable.[3]

Attorneys representing treaty tribes were among the first to receive news of the Court's decision and spread the word by telephone. At GLIFWC's central office, staff members gathered for a pipe ceremony and talking circle, reflecting on the many ways in which a host of individuals contributed to the effort.[4]

For treaty fishermen the news was timely. In a few short weeks, ice on Minnesota 1837 lakes would melt, ushering in a brief spring harvest opportunity. Like the inaugural court-protected spring season one year earlier, all six Wisconsin bands and Fond du Lac joined Mille Lacs in taking fish by net and spear from Lake Mille Lacs.

Tobasonakwut Kinew smudges a chain of prayer sticks with sage at Sandy Lake in March 1999. COR

Closing the circle

While the justices of the Supreme Court were mulling over the *Minnesota v. Mille Lacs* case in early 1999, tribal officials fixed their energies on coming to terms with the Sandy Lake tragedy. The insidious episode which claimed the lives of four hundred Ojibwe people 148 years earlier had been largely excluded from oral histories and overlooked by most academics. It was time to recognize the sacrifice Ojibwe people made at Sandy Lake.

Assisted by Tobasonakwut Kinew—who served as a spiritual leader during the Waabanong Run—representatives from Ojibwe bands in Wisconsin, Minnesota and Michigan gathered on a small glacial knoll overlooking Sandy Lake for a closure ceremony. Situated in the northwest corner of the lake, this same land witnessed the annuity death gathering many decades earlier. The Ojibweg that assembled there now sought to bring peace to the spirits of those who suffered and died on the frozen ground.

A ceremonial fire was lit, food prepared, and prayer sticks constructed of carved and painted maple were given to each community representative with instructions to decorate and display the sticks in their tribal offices. Mille Lacs' Little Otter Drum played a series of songs and Kinew spoke at length in both English and Ojibwemowin inside a circle formed by whites and tribal members.

Jim Clark, an elder from Mille Lacs, spoke and guided the placement of an eagle feather onto a nearby tree. As the ceremony neared completion, everyone danced, laughter drifted through the bare trees, over the resting places, and to the sky. Kinew said that the Ojibwe ancestors would hear these cheerful voices and find comfort.[5]

Before departing for a feast at Mille Lacs, a chain of spirit sticks identical to those bound for tribal centers was released into the nearby Sandy River as people whispered prayers for the fallen along the river bank and sprinkled tobacco into the cool springtime water.

A closure ceremony for the spirits at Sandy Lake included drum songs, dancing and a feast. COR

They are remembered— ### *Mikwendaagoziwag*

The ceremony that took place on the last day of March 1999 increased awareness of the Sandy Lake tragedy in Ojibwe communities around the region. Under the direction of the Voigt Intertribal Task Force, GLIFWC staff began discussing how to appropriately preserve the memory of the Sandy Lake victims so they would never again be forgotten. By autumn that year, GLIFWC staff initiated a dialogue with the Wisconsin and Minnesota State Historical Societies, along with the United States Army Corps of Engineers, a federal agency that administers the property surrounding the Sandy Lake dam where the closure ceremony was held. All parties agreed that details of the 1850 annuity payment had received little historical attention and should

An archeological team examines the proposed Mikwendaagoziwag Memorial site. Animal bone, arrowheads and pottery shards were uncovered, but no evidence of human burials were found. COR

Tribal members place commemorative stones into the concrete pedestal of the Mikwendaagoziwag Memorial. Four hundred stones representing the Ojibweg who died in 1850-51 were collected from Ojibwe communities in Wisconsin, Upper Michigan and Minnesota. SE

be presented to the public through an interpretive roadside marker.

Over the following months, writers from the different organizations outlined, wrote, and reworked text for a historical marker destined to be placed at the Highway 65 wayside near Brown's Point and the location of the 1850 annuity payment.

While continuing to develop the marker, tribal elders and leaders expressed the need to establish a memorial or monument for their ancestors; properly caring for the spirits of those who suffered and died was fundamental to Ojibwe culture and society. With the cooperation of the Army Corps, a workgroup of GLIFWC staff, tribal representatives, and elders planned for the 150th anniversary of the Sandy Lake annuity payment, including a permanent memorial and commemorative run. The glacial mound situated at the Army Corps' public recreation area was selected to shoulder the *Mikwendaagoziwag* (they are remembered) Memorial, and workgroup participants traveled to sites around Wisconsin in search of a suitable monument stone. They found it in the southern corner of the 1842 ceded territory—a two-ton red granite boulder that had been quarried near Mountain, Wis. Standing more than six feet high, the bottom portion of the boulder was trimmed off, creating a flat surface that could be attached to a low pedestal. As for the smaller end-piece, tribal representatives decided it should be delivered to Madeline Island.

While GLIFWC's Jim Zorn took the lead in coordinating construction and design of the monument, archeologists conducted a formal excavation of the glacial knoll near the shore of Sandy Lake. A similar mound nearby was dotted with the graves of American Indians and settlers, prompting the investigation to prevent disturbing a burial site. Elise Aune, Mille Lacs Cultural Resources Compliance Officer, worked alongside a crew of four archeologists, meticulously sifting down through layers of soil. Arrowheads and pottery shards originating from precontact native people to European immigrants were uncovered along with animal bone. The location where the monument would rest appeared to simply be an occupation site, and Army Corps Archeologist Brad Johnson submitted approval for construction to begin.[6]

From October 2000 into the following year, the monument was pieced together in stages, beginning with the construction of a concrete pedestal embellished with 400 small grandfather stones; the stones—collected from reservation communities—represented those who died generations earlier. The red granite boulder was fixed to the pedestal, followed by the placement of bronze plaques recognizing the nineteen annuity bands along with the 12 present-day reservations which their descendants call home. A slice of pipestone offered by Fran Van Zile served as a place to put down tobacco.

Cutting the red granite monument stone in Mosinee, Wis. Krukowski Stone Company *prepared the two-ton boulder used in memorials at Sandy Lake and Madeline Island.* JZ

Staff from Mille Lacs, St. Croix and GLIFWC position the monument stone on the Mikwendaagoziwag Memorial. COR

A firekeeper's experience: "The air suddenly got still"

Leo LaFernier lights a sacred fire at Sandy Lake in 1999. COR

The people involved in memorializing the Ojibwe who suffered and died in 1850-51 were determined to do things the proper way. Elders and spiritual leaders from across Ojibwe Country were consulted and monthly meetings were held. The great discussion that rose from the process was thorough and inclusive.

For many human beings—regardless of culture or religion—spiritual validation can be hard to come by. Am I doing this ceremony correctly? Am I making a connection? Deep into a clear October night, Red Cliff elder Leo LaFernier received an answer.

LaFernier and members of his family are well-known as firekeepers. During ceremonial events, like the four day fire that preceded the Supreme Court hearing in Washington DC, he is often involved in 'round-the-clock' maintenance of the flames. In early October 2000, LaFernier and his grandson Donald Carlson arranged and tended a sacred fire at Sandy Lake where construction was beginning on the Mikwendaagoziwag Memorial. Before leaving his Red Cliff home for Sandy Lake, LaFernier had dismissed a "very loud and insistent knock" at his front door that produced no apparent visitor. An encounter the following evening, however, caused him to rethink the event. After thoughtful consideration, LaFernier described how it happened.

October 9-10, 2000: Sandy Lake, Minnesota

[We] lined the fire pit with cedar and sage, and at 7:20 a.m. as the sun rose over the lake, we lit the fire and performed [a] sunrise ceremony, using the elements of sage, sweet grass, tobacco and water. We asked the Creator to bless the area and included that area of the mound where the monument is to be constructed.

[That evening] Donald and I sat around talking for some time. Then I decided I would go into the truck and get some rest while he watched the fire. I got up at 2:30 a.m. to relieve Don and talked a while, then he went to rest. The sky was clear with almost a full moon, shining bright, the temperature was mild. At about 3:15 a.m. the fire was burning but not bright, as I had not added wood for some time. It seemed that the air suddenly got still and I sensed or thought I heard something. The lake is big and noise carries a long way across water so I dismissed it out of my mind. Then I heard what sounded like a shuffling of many feet across the grass. It seemed to come from the direction of the river [Sandy River], then from behind me, then from the mound. I knew I was being visited.

As I stood by the fire praying in every humble way not knowing what was expected of me it occurred to me that I should be calm and unafraid as I was in the circle of the sacred fire. It seemed to me then it got very still and quiet, then a noise on the water, almost like the sound of a beaver tail only more muffled. I arranged my chair in the doorway [an opening in the ring of cedar and sage that surrounded the fire] facing the East. Giving thanks to the Creator for this experience although I did not understand, I asked for guidance.

After I completed my pipe ceremony, I was calm but confused and overwhelmed, so I sat directing my thoughts to the fire. As I rehashed the events of that day I remembered that insistent knock at my door early that morning warning me I was going to be late. It occurred to me after connecting the early event and the later that it was right for me to be here.

Again, I sensed a presence right behind me. I glanced toward my shadow [and saw] nothing, but knew there was a presence there. Without turning I reached down, picked up tobacco, sage and cedar [and] walked to the fire and made an offering. Then I said aloud "Boozhoo, na bah da bin" [Hello, come in, sit down]. As I stood by the fire looking down I could feel a presence enter the doorway circle of the fire [and] then exit. I stayed at the fire for some time, not looking up. How much time lapsed during this episode is uncertain, but I think about one hour.

The Mikwendaagoziwag Run

Bearing their sick and enough food for a couple of days, Ojibwe families trudged off in just about every direction away from Sandy Lake following the partial annuity payment completed on December 2, 1850. To commemorate this grueling wintertime journey—which became a death march for hundreds—tribal planners agreed that a Waabanong-style run from Sandy Lake to Madeline Island was appropriate. Home of the Ojibwe Nation and traditional location for annuity payments, the Island would receive the thankful prayers carried in the hearts and minds of each participant. Although it may have not been apparent to the Wisconsin Ojibwe who spurned removal 150 years earlier, their sacrifice on the trails from Sandy Lake made it possible for future generations to live upon the Ojibwe homelands south of Lake Superior.

Sun rising over Sandy Lake December 2, 2000. COR

As an assembly of people came together at Mille Lacs for feasting, smudging and ceremonies, firekeepers sparked a sacred flame at Ojibway Memorial Park on Madeline Island. The small, mostly open town park protects the grave of Buffalo's 1852 companion to Washington, Chief Oshoga, after the Red Cliff Band and local supporters thwarted a condominium development project in the mid-1980s. Over a four day period, firekeepers from Red Cliff and Bad River would maintain the fire until the commemorate runners arrived from Sandy Lake.[7]

A pink dawn cut through frosted trees on December 2, 2000 along the east shore of Sandy Lake as a host of people gathered near a fire at the foot of the newly erected Mikwendaagoziwag

THE WHITE HOUSE
WASHINGTON

November 29, 2000

Warm greetings to the members of the Lake Superior Chippewa Indians as you gather to commemorate the 150th anniversary of the Sandy Lake Tragedy in Minnesota.

This solemn occasion reminds all Americans of a dark chapter in our country's history, when thousands of Chippewa suffered -- and hundreds died -- from illness, hunger, and exposure in the winter of 1850, far from their homes and families. By coming together to remember your ancestors who lost their lives during this terrible event, you are beginning the process of healing and reconciliation and helping a new generation of Americans to learn from one of our country's most tragic mistakes.

I am pleased to know that the Army Corps of Engineers is working with your tribes to build an enduring monument to all those who suffered and died at Sandy Lake. I join you in paying tribute to the memory of your ancestors, and I extend best wishes to all for a meaningful ceremony.

Bill Clinton

Letter from President Bill Clinton. GLIFWC

Prayer stick in hand, Fran Van Zile leads a group of Mikwendaagoziwag walkers through McGregor, Minn. COR

Elizabeth Martin, Nick Van Der Puy and Josh Van Zile running east from the St. Louis River. COR

Monument. The snow covered earth and biting four-below-zero temperature stirred the imaginations of those pondering that same day many generations ago when Ojibwe people began walking home—their canoes useless on the frozen waterways. Tobasonakwut Kinew presided over the sunrise ceremony and the Little Otter Drum sang healing and traveling songs.

Twenty-six individuals had showed up for the run of remembrance, including Waabanong core runners Joel Shagobay, Don Graves, Jim Schlender and Neil Kmiecik. Before the Run started, a spirit dish containing fish, fruit and asemaa was lowered into the fire, offering sustenance to the souls who had walked on. The gathering shared a light breakfast and drew up relay rotations for the walkers and runners. Shoulder pins made of ribbons and cedar were distributed along with additional cedar sprigs for the runners' shoes.

Late in the morning as the sun crested in the clear sky, Shagobay began the Run carrying one of four talking sticks crafted for the occasion by Red Cliff's Marvin DeFoe. Each talking stick was adorned with colored ribbons—red, yellow, white, and blue—emblematic of the four directions. During talking circles, while running, and at fireside ceremonies the talking sticks were utilized throughout the next three days.[8]

After a dozen southerly miles, the Run turned east at McGregor where state Highway 210 featured comparably wide shoulders. Walkers and runners began traveling in groups, those with more strength encouraging the others, a symbolic act of the truly difficult experience long ago. Like much of upper Minnesota, the terrain featured flat marshland and bogs, drained by streaming waterways and shallow lakes. Small random hayfields rose from the wet earth where optimistic farmers had cleared the land of trees. Crossing this country in the nineteenth century was challenging by canoe and extremely arduous on foot.[9]

Near the eastern edge of the Fond du Lac reservation, the run tapered off after 50-odd miles. Night was setting in and the runners and walkers formed a talking circle in the Black Bear Hotel. It was an emotional time as participants reflected on "what those people endured during their journey."[10] After everyone had the opportunity to speak, they broke for dinner and found lodging in homes and hotels in the surrounding communities of Carlton and Cloquet. For some, the luxuries of full stomachs and warm, dry beds seemed inappropriate.

The wild beauty of Jay Cooke State Park enveloped the Mikwendaagoziwag company the next morning as they wound their way through the St. Louis River basin. The steep, serpentine road was lined with looming hardwoods broken only by stands of evergreens and stocky red cedar trees. People stopped to put down tobacco at various spots along the historic water route, including the starting point of the Grand Portage where early travelers entering from Lake Superior pulled their canoes from the St. Louis and carried them overland around a long series of rapids and waterfalls.[11]

Crossing the old Oliver wooden bridge, runners carried a pair of talking sticks into Wisconsin. Further east, walkers were traveling narrow roads south of Superior, bound for State Highway 13. As in the Waabanong Run, leap-frogging segments of road between walkers and runners allowed participants of any endurance level to take part throughout the day. Upon emerging from the St. Louis River valley, the gusting westerly winds grew more pronounced, pressing the Run toward Madeline Island. Miles passed quickly as they trekked along Lake Superior's south shore until halting near Port Wing.

By noon the following day, the Mikwendaagoziwag Run had advanced to Red Cliff where participants and supporters assembled to cover the last few miles together. Once in Bayfield people boarded a ferry and motored across the choppy emerald water to the village of La Pointe. A dozen Ojibwe and non-Indians hit the Madeline Island dock running and carried the talking sticks and staffs through town and to the sacred fire at Ojibway Memorial Park. A ring of cedar boughs circled the fire with a break—a doorway—to the east left open. Here,

Crossing the Oliver bridge in December 2000, Larry Nesper, Graham Zorn and Neil Kmiecik run with a pair of prayer sticks crafted for the Mikwendaagoziwag Run. COR

Runners joined a gathering of people for a ceremony around the sacred fire on Madeline Island on December 4, 2000. Firekeepers on Madeline Island tended a four-day fire while runners and walkers traveled east from Sandy Lake. COR

Through this we connect with our ancestors and become more involved in the meaning of the treaties—the human elements—not just hunting and fishing. It is respecting what they did for us today.

Fred Ackley
Sokaogon Ojibwe
December 4, 2000

holding tobacco, ceremony participants crossed into a spiritually protected place and walked clockwise around the fire, distributing their offering to the Creator over the flames.

The growing power of the west wind rocked nearby trees and surging white-capped waves slammed into the shoreline. Sweat-soaked runners absorbed the penetrating wind, the discomfort serving to fuel the veneration many felt toward those determined to walk a hundred miles—some four times that number—just to get back home. Sokaogon's Robert Van Zile led the closing ceremony and a handful of individuals added words and prayer. Pipes were passed; people were smudged with sage, and the Bad River Youth Drum played honor songs for the dead. The message to the spirits was clear—the Ojibwe of 1850 would always be remembered. Mikwendaagoziwag.

Notes: Chapter Five

[1] *Outdoor News* (Wis.), Dec. 18, 1999, "Wisconsin AG, Crist differ on High Court's comments," 1; *Masinaigan,* Spring 1999, "Whichever way the Court rules," 4.

[2] *Masinaigan,* "Whichever way the court rules."

[3] *Minnesota v. Mille Lacs,* 119 S.Ct. 1187 (1999), 1192, 1198.

[4] *Masinaigan,* Summer 1999, "March 24, 1999—A good day in Indian Country," 2.

[5] *Masinaigan,* Summer 1999, "Sandy Lake, Minnesota: Remembering a Dark Chapter in Ojibwe History," 16.

[6] This information from my notes taken while observing the excavation.

[7] Richard Jack, Francis Leoso, Butch Stone and Gilmore Wilson served as firekeepers.

[8] Both black and blue are used to represent "South."

[9] Minnesota Department of Natural Resources, "The Savanna Portage." Three page typescript.

[10] *Masinaigan Supplement,* Spring 2001, 7.

[11] John Fritzen. "Portages & Old Trails Inland and Adjacent to Jay Cooke State Park," 1935.

Epilogue

The Mikwendaagoziwag Memorial was formally dedicated in July 2001, drawing scores of tribal members, U.S. Army Corps of Engineers representatives, a handful of local residents, and Great Lakes Indian Fish & Wildlife Commission staff who hosted the event. While most people arrived on Sandy Lake's west shore in motor vehicles, a fleet of canoes carried additional participants to the Memorial, culminating a commemorative water and land journey from Madeline Island known as *Ondakwazhiwe Kekiwed Inakwazhiwe.*

While some destinations on the great Ojibwe Journey have been reached, there remain vast distances to cover. The long road to achieve legal protection for rights reserved in treaties with the United States has been realized by many Ojibwe tribes in the Lake Superior region; nevertheless, anti-Indian groups maintain their commitment to eliminate tribal sovereignty. Elders and educators struggle to keep Ojibwemowin from fading; novelties of the modern world distract young tribal members from traditional endeavors like wild plant gathering and fishing. Ojibwe people have demonstrated in the late twentieth century that remembering ancestors, events and lifeways is an active, engaging venture. For as long as tribal members keep their makizinan laced-up, the Ojibwe Journey will advance far into the future.

The Mikwendaagoziwag Memorial. COR

APPENDIX A
Waabanong Run Journal
(Sketch of Running Route by Day)

By Neil Kmiecik and Jim Schlender
November 11-27, 1998

Nov. 11—Day 1 (Wednesday) Lac du Flambeau to Merrill, Wisconsin

"Shortly after sunrise a pipe ceremony was held at the Lac du Flambeau Bear River Pow-wow grounds. Runners were smudged, put tobacco in the fire and said prayers for the families they were leaving behind. They were taught a pipe loading song and then smoked two pipes one of which had its bowl shaped like a walleye; this pipe was given to Mille Lacs by the Lakota. An eagle sat nearby the Bear River and flew with the leaders and elders as they walked with the staff to the highway. Runners and walkers then began relaying the staff; they were outfitted with ribbons and an eagle feather pinned to their left shoulder. Winds were brisk out of the west signifying that spirits from the west were with and watching over the core group. Other eagles and many deer were seen along the route. Runners made good time despite a thin layer of ice crusted snow along the shoulder. Aided by Gary "Kemo" Kmiecik, Bob Jackson, Tobasonakwut, Kekek, and Ernie St. Germaine the core group was able to cover about 66 miles and reached Merrill shortly after dark.

A talking circle was held. Kemo said he could only run today; his good words about the veterans feather tied to the staff carried by walkers and his strong spirit will be missed. Tobasonakwut wanted to stay but hurried back to Minneapolis to finish work on a runners pipe so that he could present it in time for Saturday's sweat lodge near Madison."

Nov. 12—Day 2 (Thursday) Merrill to Plover, Wisconsin

Runners and walkers gathered in a corner of the motel parking lot just before sunrise. They were smudged and told to think about Supreme Court Justice Anthony Kennedy in their prayers as they ran. They were given t-shirts, hats, and Waabanong Run signs for their vehicles. People loaded into their vehicles went to the point where the run stopped the previous night and began running. After a couple hours people began talking about food so Jim

Schlender went into town and loaded up with fruit, sandwich meat and breads. Everyone was happy when he came back.

A little past Wausau a Channel 9 TV news crew filmed runners and walkers and did an interview with Jim. We saw the news piece on TV in the evening and everyone was pleased with the coverage; we all laughed when we saw the Mille Lacs ninja running. Gil Halstead caught up with us and gave us a tape with the pipe-loading song received earlier and Erik Gahbow and others listened carefully to the song to learn it. During our evening talking circle Erik and Budman led us in this song.

We ran and walked a little over 60 miles and finished at the junction of Hoover Avenue and Prairie Road about 5 miles south of Plover. We're almost out of the ceded territory, the landscape has changed from wooded to more urban and agricultural. We ended around 4:15 and drove back to Jean Day's house in Stevens Point. We smoked the pipe, were smudged, and had a talking circle. We then ate corn soup, apple pie and ice cream. We were joined after supper by students with AIRO and AISES from UW-Stevens Point, Jim Hudson, Billy Jo Grimm, Andy Gokee.

Nov. 13—Day 3 (Friday) Plover to Portage, Wisconsin

Woke up to the aroma and sounds of bacon and sausage sputtering in the pan. Jean Day our hostess arrived late in the evening after everyone had gone to bed and woke early before anyone arose to prepare breakfast. As she cooked we lingered in memories of old friendships laughing and teasing as Ho Chunk, Lakota, and Anishinabeg commonly do. After breakfast we loaded up the vehicles and gathered together in a circle. Jean smudged everyone and gave each a tobacco tie from Ho Chunk ceremonies. She said she would pray for us each day. She reminded us that like Sundancers every step upon the earth and on our journey is a prayer. To assist us she gave us some bitterroot, plus another Indian medicine that once saved her brother from a gunshot wound when Western medicine failed, and some cedar. The runners were asked to pray for Supreme Court Justice Sandra Day O'Connor and her family. Four geese flew overhead traveling south and then turned east, a symbol of the path we were undertaking. Several of us felt sad to leave such a good friend.

We started running around 7:30. Billy Jo Grimm was first to run and Andy Gokee donated some money. Andy, Holly, Mita, and Billy Jo seemed sad that they had to leave and probably wished they could stay. Randy had an arch injury and after the first mile spent time resting but felt better later and ran a couple more miles. Charlie developed knee pains yesterday and they didn't get better overnight. He ran one mile but decided it would be smarter to walk the rest of the day. Kemo joined us and contributed four miles before heading to St. Louis. Don Graves received word that his mother-in-law had died and returned to Minneapolis with Bob Jackson. We wished Don well and asked him to come back if he could. We thanked Bob for his help and support; to us he represented the U.S. who also is a party in the case before the Supreme Court.

We felt the trickster's influence around Coloma and Packwaukee. In Coloma the map was mislabeled and we found it difficult to know where all of us were. Jim and Charlie lost the runners but found them by following the sun. As it happens sometimes, a good outcome occurred when the route we took ended up being shorter than the one we had mapped out. As the miles added up our legs began to tire, and we missed the contributions of all the runners that had already left us. But our spirits were lifted when Paul Kmiecik found us about 20 miles north of Portage and ran 2 five mile legs at speeds greater than we were accustomed to. After talking to coworkers we once again realized all the effort that they and others were putting into this run and prayer. We were told that the ribbon shirts were done and along with eagle feathers, ribbons, and additional maps were being sent to us.

It was a beautiful day to run and walk as the temperatures climbed into the middle forties. We knew the spirits were watching us as we saw some geese in fields and others walking on lightly frozen ponds. We saw a swan and Bo played with a hawk as he ran and it circled above him. As the runners ended their journey for the day just outside of Portage at sunset, an eagle appeared and flew into the south. We had covered about 70 miles.

Some people were hungry and went out to eat right away. The rest of us held a talking circle. The pipe and everyone was smudged. We left a window and the door open and talked. Just as the last person was finishing talking, a hotel employee knocked on the door and said he had several calls from guests complaining of the smoke in the hall and that there was a funny odor. He said it smelled like marijuana and asked if that could be. We said no and he left. A minute later two policemen came upstairs and walked through the hallway.

We met for dinner at 6:30 and were joined later by a couple of those who had eaten earlier. One of them said he saw the police cars in front of the motel doors. He said he entered the lobby and as he stood near the front desk knew why the police were there. He could smell the sage. He thought that some of the runners must be upstairs getting really spiritual and they had had a fierce smudging.

Nov. 14—Day 4 (Saturday) Portage to Janesville, Wisconsin

Assembled outside of motel around 6:30 surrounded by a light fog with mist thick in the air. We decided to pray for Chief Justice Rhenquist today. Runners were reminded that the pains of exertion were part of the sacrifice and might help to make our prayers heard by the Creator. They were also asked to check that eagle feathers were tied tightly because one was lost yesterday from a walking staff.

Runners seemed to cover the distance rapidly and reached Madison before noon. We ran past farm fields and only a few wooded lots which was a landscape much different than the wilderness experienced by John Muir when walking this same path nearly 150 years ago. Erik turned his ankle but was able to keep running. While Eva was running a couple of large farm tractors came by hugging the shoulder but veered out onto the roadway to go by her. Jim aggravated two old injuries by sprinting across two intersections in Madison and then having to run further than he had planned.

Jim left around noon to meet Patty Lowe and to replace his lost glasses. The runners and walkers continued to chew up the miles but a food run was needed to replenish the supply of sandwich meat, bread and power bars. Runners grabbed sandwiches, ran through Stoughton and arrived in Edgerton around 2:30. Some runners then decided to rest for the day but others continued and arrived in Janesville around 4:30 just as it was beginning to get dark. John Coleman caught up with the runners in this stretch and ran hard for a mile.

Runners that developed injuries were checked at Patty's by Dr. Peter Hanson. He intended to help provide relief for blisters but no one had any. Instead he told people how to care for their particular injury. Mitch Soulier stopped by and dropped off ribbon shirts, maps, antlers, and feathers. Art Shegonee had spent several days reconstructing the sweat lodge and together with the fire keeper they had everything ready for a sweat soon after dark.

A fruit salad was served and a spirit dish prepared. Persons intending to sweat then walked down to the lodge and put their tobacco in the fire. The pipe loading song was sung and three pipes loaded. Tobasonakwut prayed and said that Mother Earth had called for the feather to return to her and said that we were supposed to let it go. After the sweat the basket given by Patty was put into the fire and we were told to pray for those that had already gone into the spirit world.

After the sweat food was served. Patty had cooked up a feast of spaghetti, apple crisp, cookies, and fresh bread. Dr. Hanson gave us a tobacco pouch with money in it. People began to find spots on the floor and elsewhere to sleep. Peter and Kekek visited for awhile and then returned to Minneapolis to continue work on the runners pipe. Patty put Jim downstairs in what we all hoped was a soundproof room. Unfortunately, he snored so loud the door rattled open and the sounds escaped.

Nov. 15—Day 5 (Sunday) Janesville, Wisconsin to Belvidere, Illinois

People began waking at various times from 5:00-8:00. Patty cooked pancakes and we had lots of juice, cider and coffee. She boiled up the medicine that Jean Day gave us, and we put it in a water container. We passed out the ribbon shirts that the staff made for the runners, and they were beautiful. We gathered on the deck and formed in a circle for the runners to be smudged. Carol Brown had just come and joined us. We were asked to pray for Supreme Court Justice Antonin Scalia today. Patty was given a Waabanong Run ribbon shirt in appreciation for her kindness and generous hospitality. She talked how this run was similar to the journey Chief Buffalo took to Washington D.C. to secure the treaties in 1850.

We left around 9:00 and met Art Shegonee on an off-ramp. He gave us a big eagle feather and told us he had talked to the Heiders' about stopping by their ranch this morning. Then we drove to Janesville and arrived at the Heiders' around 10:20. We shook hands with Dave and he gave us an offering which we tied to the staff. We walked back by where Miracle was kept and held a ceremony. From the moment it started until the moment it ended, Miracle stood right behind us, facing the circle, and looking our way.

We drove to our starting point and began running after 11:00. Gene Connor walked the last mile in Wisconsin and took a wrong turn right away in Illinois. We got back on track and ran to Roscoe. There was road construction, and as we were sitting in the median a police car stopped behind us with his lights flashing. He inquired about how many runners we had and he kindly offered to stop traffic as we crossed a busy intersection. We continued running and when it was Eva's turn she was greeted by a pack of collies which fortunately were behind a fence.

As the runners continued towards Belvidere Jim went to find rooms. We arrived in town around 4:30. Seven runners wanted to keep going and in the next two hours reached Highway 23. Upon their return, we gathered for a talking circle. While smudging the runners and smoking the pipe, the smoke detector went off and we had a hard time figuring out how to stop it. We laughed about our ineptitude later. We went to supper and then Paul, Conan, and Carol returned to Madison. They were thanked for their contribution and friendship and will be missed. This marked a day of change for us because we now have no one else to supplement our efforts.

Nov. 16—Day 6 (Monday) Belvidere to Marseilles, Illinois

Sunrise ceremony around 7:00 am in motel parking lot in Belvidere. Stopped for food and coffee and then drove around 14 miles to starting point. Road was dirt and gravel for awhile. Jim's car started to overheat; Neil and Francis went back to the creek & filled up some bottles and a jug and the problem was temporarily solved. Jim went to DeKalb and got some "Stop Leak" which took care of it. He picked up some asema from an India-Indian tobacconist. Bo ran through downtown but missed the turn. Jim caught him before he went too far in the wrong direction and then went to pick him some additional maps at the NIU bookstore. Larry bought some bargain sunglasses in town; Joel told him that they made his eyes look like they were on upside down.

Ran to the south and into a moderate breeze down Hwy 23. Quite a bit of truck traffic and as they flew by we braced ourselves in their draft. Gene said he walked a mile-and-a-half in his one mile leg because he went back to pick up his hat so many times. Picked up water near Waterman and more sandwich meat in town near Sandwich.

While Jim was doing his walk between two branches of Little Indian Creek, the road dipped down underneath a railroad trestle. He had just said his Anishinaabe name and clan; just as he started to pray for Justice John Paul Stevens he distinctly heard an Indian Song coming from high up in the trees along the road. Later when he crossed this creek, he stopped and put asemaa in ziibing and said thank you for this wondrous sign.

Continued south and walkers crossed the Fox River while runners continued on to Marseilles and stopped at the Illinois River just at dark. Neil took Francis back to Chicago, he was the last of the runners called "new horses coming our way" to leave. The core runners named the van that these runners rode in "Bebezhigooganzhii" which means "one big toenail" or horse in English. The other two vans returned to Ottawa to stay overnight at two different locations. We didn't have a talking circle because not everyone was present. Charlie met his friend Garth and after supper they headed back to Yorkville and on to Sparta the next day. Charlie said he was going to wear his Waabanong Run shirt on November 28th and December 2nd in honor of the runners. He gave a lot of himself to others and to the run; walking helped him work through the injury to his knees and on this day he both ran and walked. Now all that remains are the core runners and walkers.

Nov. 17—Day 7 (Tuesday) Marseilles to Chatsworth, Illinois

Checked out of motel in Ottawa and held ceremony near bridge over the Illinois river in Marseilles. We were happy to see Gene and Eva because we had gotten disconnected the previous evening. Bo, the first runner, ran up and over the bridge while a hawk flew towards the south over a farm field. Neil had a long uphill on his first leg and beat a truck hauling two large fertilizer containers up it. Bo cracked up over a Halloween witch display which suggested that she wasn't watching where she was going and crashed into a telephone pole. Larry ran by some people roofing a house and one of them yelled "wash-tay" at him, which means "good" in Lakota. When runners were asked if they were a "horse" today, both Budman and Erik said they were.

A little later Eva was running down a gravel road when a horse ran to the corner of it's corral and stood looking her way. As she moved past, it jumped in an excited way and dashed to the other end of the corral where it continued to stand looking at her. When we were at the Heider's ranch the buffalo born as a white buffalo calf and named Miracle stood looking at us while we prayed with the pipe and held a ceremony. Birds from different nations have looked our way as we've run by; today a flock that looked like black leaves standing up on the branches, chirped and sung from a distant grove of trees to the east of us. In other places, horses have stood watching us. When these things happen we feel that our journey has meaning and that the animal nations are looking our way.

On a couple of occasions there was no road so runners took off across the countryside running towards the zhaawanong giizis rather than run three or more miles out of the way. A narrow footbridge hidden in the woods crossed one of these rivers. A runner crossed a shallow rapids area of the other river, then through a wooded lot, around a dry creek bed, and up a hill to the road. We talked about the importance of doing extra-ordinary things at times. Budman ran a two mile leg and said he felt a need to be on this run because his mother's father is from Mille Lacs. Randy continued to run in a determined way despite some injuries that haven't quite gone away.

During the day several policemen stopped and inquired in a friendly manner about what we were doing. We gave them a copy of our press release and one said he'd pass it "down the line." We stopped going south near Chenowah and started running Waabanong on Highway 24. We stopped just outside of Forrest around sunset. We drove to Gilman and checked into a motel near the interstate.

Nov. 18—Day 8 (Wednesday) Chatsworth, Illinois to Remington, Indiana

Watched sunrise and had ceremony in the sunshine on lawn behind motel in Gillman. Today we were to pray for Supreme Court Justice Stephen Breyer and his family. A flock of geese flew by heading south. A sheet listing the runner/walker rotation was given to each vehicle; written at the bottom was something to consider, i.e. "Like the spotted lizard, a warrior must be adaptable and creative—ready to change on a moments notice."

Drove back to Chatsworth where the run ended last night and began running a little before 8:00; it was cold at first but after about an hour it warmed up. Jim continued to have radiator trouble and Mitch got water from a nearby creek for it. The gravel shoulder along the road was very narrow and all day trucks speeding by on Highway 24 blasted the runners and the staff with wind gusts. Eva's arm got tired by the end of the day from these blasts. Gene told Jim that he probably wouldn't have a problem with the wind but Gene would have to put extra change in his pocket to keep from being blown away. During Randy's first mile a truck came really close and sprayed gravel on him. This made him angry and he started walking for a short ways. At the end of his mile he put some tobacco down and the anger left him. After Eva finished her first mile Jim noticed some bird poop on the sleeve of her windbreaker and said that the birds nations were not only looking down upon her but sending her messages. During Erik and Joel's first mile they wore black face masks which made them look like Ninja terrorists but to us they were simply Ninjuns.

Around 9:00 we discovered that we had started in the wrong spot; we should have started just outside of Forrest. So Neil, Bo, Joe Dan, and Mitch went back to make up this six mile stretch. As they approached they could see Forrest through the fields. Joe Dan said we were like tail dancers. The lesson of the spotted lizard was expressed.

Runners and walkers moved fast all morning and for awhile each of our three staffs was being used. Jim heard a high pitched chorus of an Indian song which sounded like women singing from a distance. We went through Gilman and then on to Watseka with runners fueled by sandwiches, power bars, and high energy drinks. Zhaawanong noodin moved swiftly and unfettered over the fields most of the day; we felt it pushing us north as we moved east. We saw a blue heron flying with one short leg and found a cardinal dead alongside the road which we kept. Joe Dan ran by some horses and they came forward as if curious and stood looking his way. Our pace slowed a little in the afternoon but we ran steady, strong, and with a good spirit; each runner covered 7-8 miles while the walkers went 4-5. Budman and Erik finished their last mile fast and strong; they have become horses.

We checked into a motel in Remington. The sun was setting and the only cloud in the southwest sky was stretched out and looked like a beautiful red-orange miigwan before turning a little later to a gray one against an orange sky. It was a good sign to end the day on. Erik led us in the pipe loading song and after smoking the pipe we held a talking circle. People mentioned how we've come together as a team and how our focus while running has become more of a prayer.

Nov. 19—Day 9 (Thursday) Remington to Marion, Indiana

A sunrise ceremony was held behind the motel in Remington around 6:30 (central time). Wind from the west blew sage out of shell so we moved behind a corner of the building and finished smudging everyone. Jim Zorn brought tobacco grown by a friend of his in Wisconsin and gave it to us. He said that when asked if he was a "horse" he answered by making a whinnying sound and suggested that this was the word of the day. He added that many people back home were interested in following the run. Tom Maulson who is following our progress on the website said there were over 900 hits last night. We were asked to pray for Supreme Court Justice Clarence Thomas and his family today.

Jim Z. volunteered to start first and run a long leg so that others could get coffee and gas up. Ningabeanong chinoodin aided runners all day and Jim finished 5 miles quickly. While others continued running, Neil took Jim back to his car and became increasingly concerned because his van wouldn't shift into third gear. Neil stopped to feed Bebezhigooganzhii (which has over 370,000 miles) with gas, oil and transmission fluid and it responded by shifting into third gear all day.

Highway 24 through Indiana has a very narrow shoulder which drops off quickly and steeply. While traveling along it we were reminded that the right road is often narrow and difficult while the wrong road is typically easy. If we had wanted to take the easy road we could have arranged to drive or fly the staff to DC.

Our daily routine includes stopping every mile or so and waiting for the runner or walker to finish their leg before handing the staff to the next person. Today everyone seemed to have a good pow-wow tape turned up loud and heads were bouncing. We crossed the Tippicanoe river in Monticello, the Wabash river in Peru, and the Eel river in Logansport. Historically, this area had many Potawatomi and Miami villages. Following land cession treaties in the 1830's this stretch of land contained over 100 small reservations. Trees and hills began to reappear which was a welcome sight after days of running over flat earth and through farm fields. As the wind mixed with the pow-wow music the different tree nations seemed to be dancing; those with leaves moved and sounded like jingle dress dancers.

Around 9:30 Piishko called from his classroom at Ball State University and asked some questions about the run. About three hours later as we were stopped at France Park, Piishko along with three of his students and a radio reporter arrived. Two vultures soared overhead and we asked if those were Indiana eagles. The reporter ran along Erik and Joel and taped their conversation. Next, Piishko ran two miles and his students Jody Huff, Tim Wright, and Paul Butler walked and ran a mile each. We found out that Don Graves was stuck in a blizzard in Bemidji and probably wouldn't be able to return to us until tomorrow. Even though weather predictions have called for rain and cold weather the past few days, we continue to be blessed with mild temper-atures (40-60's). Hearing of the blizzard makes us appreciate what we've been given even more.

Mitch and Ninjun Joel warmed up for their first mile by doing a short ren-dition of a men's traditional dance. Later on Ninjun Joel was attacked by the van's metal door. As he put ice above his eye, we wondered if we needed to send him back to Ninja school. Ninjun Erik, Budman, and Bo each seemed to breeze through their seven miles.

We ran and walked hard today. We covered about 70 miles by 3:00 pm and still needed to go another 20 before reaching Marion. The trickster must have messed with our maps when we were estimating mileage; our daily goal was to have been around 60-65 miles. Nevertheless, Erik and others wanted to keep going and everyone's energy was still strong. Without the walkers who covered around 30 miles altogether we wouldn't have been able to reach Marion. Jim Schlender, Joe Dan, Mitch, and Gene walked their fastest miles so far and covered five miles each.

We reached Marion around 6:00 pm (central time) and drove back to Peru where the Miami Nation of Indians opened their tribal center to us. We sang the pipe loading song, had a pipe ceremony, and a talking circle. Everyone recognized that we had accomplished something unexpected and extra-ordi-nary today; we had done this as a team. The enthusiasm was contagious and everyone's individual effort encouraged others. We were served a hot meal and made to feel welcome. Brenda Hartleroad said she was glad to have such a determined group stay with them.

Nov. 20—Day 10 (Friday) Marion, Indiana to Greenville, Ohio

The geneaologist for the Miami tribe started biscuits and gravy breakfast around 5:00 am. People began rising from army cots around 5:30 and ate breakfast. Had ceremony around 6:45; asema and cedar were passed. Said goodbye to tribal hosts and gave them some wild rice. Piishko and Jim Zorn started running while others gassed up and got coffee.

Ran east out of Marion and covered around 50 miles before reaching the Ohio border around 1:30 (central time). Took a group picture at the Ohio State sign. Most people ran or walked from 6-7 miles; after covering 90 miles yes-terday and running for around 1.5 hours past sunset, we were all tired. We stopped in Greenville, Ohio around sunset after covering another 25 miles.

Greenville is the site where the first treaty between the U.S. and the Chippewa was signed in 1795. Other tribes also signed this treaty including Miamis, Kickapoo, Kaskaskia, Ottawa, Potawatomi, and Delawares. At the site where the fire for this treaty gathering burned, a group of Indian people from this area and the Celina Indian Center feasted us and a youth drum sang three songs. We checked into a motel to rest and clean up.

Nov. 21—Day 11 (Saturday) Greenville to Columbus, Ohio

Sunrise ceremony in motel parking lot in Greenville, Ohio. Yesterday we were asked to pray for Supreme Court Justice David Souter; this morning we weren't asked to pray for any of the justices and found out later that we already had prayed for all nine.

Our friends from Greenville dropped off two shopping bags of fruit at the motel. The night before they also gave us a box with perhaps 50 baloney and cheese sandwiches, many bags of potato chips, cookies and soda. We all snacked on this food during the day, and it helped keep us going.

We reviewed the planned route with "kempjarz" who suggested we take Highway 571 which looked like it would be a shorter route to Springfield and Highway 40, the National Road. We drove to the site of Fort Greenville and took several group pictures. We started running about 9:00 (eastern time) and the weather was beautiful for running, cool (34 degrees), light wind, and mostly overcast. We feel blessed with the weather we've been given. The miles went by quickly as runners and walkers had three staffs going. Larry has been forced to walk the past couple of days because his knees aren't working right anymore. At one point Ninjun Joel was running by a farm and a small dog came out yipping. Ninjun Joel gave it some sort of a mysterious stare, and the dog turned around and turned into soup. We were amazed and decided he didn't need to go back to the cooking class in Ninja school.

Jim did a phone interview with WOJB around noon as part of the morning fire program. He talked about the who, what, where, when, and why of the Waabanong Run. He also talked about having the Ogichidaa on each reservation use their drums and pipes during the time that the Supreme Court arguments are being heard (9:00-10:00 central time on December 2) so that their power can be directed in prayer towards a good outcome. We hope to be drumming and singing in DC at this time also.

We entered Springfield just before 2:00 eastern time. As we got to the edge of town about an hour later, Joe Dan and Mitch found us. They had stayed as long as they could so we said goodbye in the parking lot of a closed Dairy Queen; Gene had said earlier that they had both walked as strong and big as they looked. We hope to see both of them in D.C. We'll miss there enthusiasm, jokes and pow-wow tapes.

We continued running down Highway 40 towards Columbus. Two polite and considerate ladies were curious about what we were doing so they stopped Jim and asked; he explained and gave them a press release. Ken

Irwin and Susan Mills caught up with us in their motorhome a few miles outside of Springfield and stayed with us till Columbus. They thought they could come up with a couple of runners to help us tomorrow. Everyone ran hard today and seemed to find a new reservoir of strength and endurance. Don Graves flew into Dayton the night before and we were all happy to see him; he came back strong and ran 8 miles. Altogether we covered around 80 miles and stopped just outside of Columbus about an hour after dark. Ohio State had beaten Michigan earlier and that might have accounted for some of the heavy evening traffic.

We drove east on Highway 70 and met Barbara Crandall and Jean McCord in Jacksontown and they led us to their ranch compound about 12 miles away. We smoked the pipe and had a talking circle. Then we were fed a delicious and generous meal of corn soup, fry bread, spaghetti and cake. We cleaned up and everyone disappeared into different rooms to rest.

Nov. 22—Day 12 (Sunday) Columbus to Cambridge, Ohio

People began waking up shortly before sunrise. Some had slept upstairs in the house. Bo slept on the living room couch; others slept in one of two motor homes that were set up for us. Jim slept outside in the tipi; it wasn't a soundproof room but it came pretty close. We laughed when he said that someone coming by during the night while he was sleeping might think there was a shaking tent ceremony going on. Frost covered everything and the dozen or so peacocks sitting like Christmas ornaments in a tree were motionless; when the sun melted the frost they flew to the ground.

Barbara Crandall, her daughter Doris, and Jean McCord were up and cooking breakfast—eggs, bacon, sweet rolls, and coffee. As people woke up they sat down in the kitchen for a plate of food and got in line for the bathroom. We visited during breakfast. We laughed when Barbara said she liked money and was a "savage for the cabbage." After breakfast, we packed up and formed into a circle outside the house in the sunlight. We were smudged and passed the staff around in a talking circle; and sang the pipe-loading song. We had already prayed for all the Supreme Court justices. Today we were asked to pray for the children of all Indian Nations so that those Nations could remain strong. Erik said that Barbara's family reminded him of his own and this helped relieve his homesickness.

We finished packing and gave rice, tobacco ties, and Waabanong Run hats to Barbara's family and friends. Dean gave us a bag full of peacock feathers. Barbara led us to a gas station where she paid for a fill-up of the vehicles. We said goodbye to them and drove to our starting points.

Jim called Ken and he said he had some runners; they agreed to start from where we stopped last night and run through Columbus, Reynoldsburg, and to a small town called Wagram. The rest of us would start from Wagram. Neil called Gary and made plans to meet. Gary and his daughter, Brook, had spent the previous day driving back and forth in Columbus looking for us before driving to Cambridge and staying the night. A dead "cell phone" zone made us unreachable for most of Saturday; it wasn't until we got into Columbus Saturday evening that the phones began working.

Jim drove back to Columbus and accompanied the runners who had driven up from Cincinnati the night before and stayed at Ken's. He explained why we were running and gave them two eagle feathers to wear. Ken said a prayer to start them off. Nathan Zimmerman then ran through two rundown sections separated by the towering buildings of the downtown. The runners took turns covering the remaining distance and ran around 22 miles altogether. A hawk soared overhead when they finished and people felt good about this.

The Waabanong runners started on Highway 40 around 9:30 (eastern time). It was a beautiful day; clear, light wind, and cool. The temperature was around 20 degrees at sunrise and rose to close to 60 by midday. Gary ran into us in Lakewood Township and started running by a "split pea soup" looking pond that he had stopped to look at yesterday. Brook wanted to walk a mile so we added her to the list of walkers. About 25 miles from Columbus the trees began returning and the hills started. Everyone got a couple of long uphill runs or walks by the end of the day.

About 10 miles east of Zanesville, the runners from Cincinnati caught up and a hawk flew nearby. They planned to head back home soon so we had a pipe ceremony and thanked them for their help. By running through town they lifted our spirits and made our task a little easier. We gave them some rice, hats and tobacco ties. A State trooper came up just as we were ending and gruffly told us to park our vehicles off the road and run on the shoulder. Most of us were unable to tune in the Green Bay vs. Minnesota football game, but we got updates of the score by various means. Erik was elated by the outcome of the game and his bets.

We ran into Cambridge at sunset. A beautiful cloud in the southwest sky moved through the sunset colors. Jim drove to get motel rooms. We took Piishko to a gas station in town where his friend from Muncie had driven to pick him up. We said goodbye and thanked Piishko for his help with running, his friendship, and for sharing his knowledge about the history of the area. Piishko often started and ended his miles by running sideways; Erik and Budman began imitating these movements in Cambridge. Budman said it was like running a football drill, then did a few steps and smilingly added that it was like a grass dance move.

Together with the Cincinnati runners we covered around 85 miles. We had a good day and felt blessed.

Nov. 23—Day 13 (Monday) Cambridge, Ohio to Washington, Pennsylvania
We met behind the motel in the parking lot next to a rock wall around 8:15 (eastern time). We were smudged and had our talking circle. Gary said we were losing running time by not being ready to run shortly after sunrise. Today we were asked to pray for the elderly. The weather was beautiful—clear and warm.

We only ran a few miles before Hwy's 40 & 70 met and combined. Gary was acting like a Heyoka (clown); while this spirit can be disruptive and irreverent it is important to acknowledge and accept because it keeps us humble and makes us laugh at ourselves. We decided to skip this 18 mile section of Interstate and drove to where Hwy 40 again split off and became the National highway just a few miles east of Morristown. We decided that we could make these miles up later. We resumed running and saw a little beagle that looked like a bagel walking down the hill so we put some chicken bones in him. Gene who was parked 10 feet behind Neil called him to see if the cell phones had started to work; Neil said his phone was ringing so Gene yelled out his van window and said to pick it up. This struck Gene as being so funny that he laughed so hard his chest began to hurt and he had to make himself stop.

It began clouding up around noon and a light mist fell for awhile. The hills continued; we laughed later about the image of big lizards running down the hills with their hands out for balance. We ran into a few obstacles. Erik had to run a two mile stretch of road that was closed because of two mobile homes that were jack-knifed across the road. Further down, the road was closed again for about a three mile stretch because of a landslide, Don ran through this stretch while vehicles had to take a detour. The front left brake on Neil's van began smoking while going downhill near Wheeling so he, Bo, and Larry spent the afternoon at a repair shop in town getting the brakes fixed. Some noticed tires, other car parts and human detritus strewn in a roadside stream. We saw a statue of a Mingo Indian made to depict the welcoming of American settlers to this area. We had never heard of the Mingo and wondered what happened to them.

Somewhere along the route we were stopped in the parking lot of a "7 Eleven" type store in West Virginia. The driver got out of his car and ran into the store but forgot to put his car in gear. Budman noticed it and yelled at the driver; he and Erik ran over and stopped it from rolling back into the road before the driver got there.

We stopped for the day in Washington which is the northern most point of Highway 40, so in one sense it's all downhill from here. But the mountains are still coming. We drove to Uniontown and waited in a parking lot of the Holiday Inn for everyone to arrive. Then we followed Delores Jones to a hunting cabin around 2500 feet up in the mountains. Her family and friends had prepared a feast of turkey, potatoes, dressing, and salad. We formed in a circle, were smudged, smoked the pipe, and had a talking circle. They had cooked a delicious meal and we thanked them for their hospitality and kindness. Some people bunked upstairs; some people drove back to stay at a motel in Uniontown, some watched the football game.

Randy thought he saw a black widow spider but couldn't get it turned over to check for a red mark. Joel, Don, and Neil woke up around 3:30 am and sat around the table and laughed until people began waking up. Don said the Mille Lacs runners had jokingly asked for capes and masks and uniforms like bobsledders and added they'd need motorcycle helmets and camouflage to run through northern Wisconsin. He told a story about trying to hock a cast-iron stove to play pull tabs at the Chicken Shack. He laughed about hocking a Gremlin for $75 to play pull tabs and then winning enough to get it out of hock. We laughed about seeing cows standing on the side of a hill and Joel saying they looked like they were having fun.

Nov 24—Day 14 (Tuesday) Washington, Pennsylvania to Frostburg, Maryland

Jim rose first around 5:30 and joined the laughing. Others slowly followed. We held our talking circle about 7:30 outside with the mountains surrounding us. We were smudged and asked to pray for the sick, incarcerated, addicted, and handicapped today. We were reminded that we are only as fast as our slowest person and that we should try to get started soon after sunrise and not an hour or so afterwards. We were cautioned about using harsh words and rough talk because the spirits were watching us. Jim offered the thought that while running to the east we were seeing more and more into this country's distant past; but at the same time many of the Indian people we have met aren't part of a recognized tribe and are struggling to maintain a connection with their Indian identity. He said that if we are not careful, what we might be seeing as Indians is our future. He asked that elders volunteer to pass on what they know and not always wait for the younger people to ask for them to share their knowledge. He also asked that the youth go to their elders and ask them to share what they know.

Delores Jones arrived with clean laundry but too late to make breakfast. She led us down the mountain and was tearful upon our departure. We started heading in the wrong direction but soon turned around and drove back to Washington. The white van was low on gas and this detour made us a little anxious. Bo had made a long-distance call the previous night and gave Jim an IOU for 18 miles as compensation. We started running and got into a rhythm and rotation where the three staffs were kept moving most of the day. We got into Uniontown around noon and began heading up the first Allegheny mountain. Eva and Neil shared the first mile and then the walkers covered the rest of this nearly 3.5 mile uphill.

The runners took over at the summit and with spirits high and strong hearts began crossing the mountains one after another. We crossed the Youghiogheny river in mid-afternoon & saw part of the original old road bridge. The water was very low and tourists were walking over the mudflats onto this bridge. Next we crossed into Maryland around 3:00. The temperature began dropping a little in the afternoon but it was still beautiful weather for running.

Gary and Jim looked at a marker along the highway and learned that in 1752 Nemacolin, a Delaware Indian, had blazed a trail. The following year General Washington used this trail to warn the French to leave the Ohio Valley. A year later General Braddock was killed by the French and while retreating his troops buried him under the road so his body wouldn't be found. This trail later became the National Highway and carried the first Anglo-Saxon settlers west of the Allegheny Mountains to what was called Fort Necessity and now is in Uniontown. Jim had the thought that we were walking along this National Pike to save the right to spear walleye pike.

We ran past sunset until around 6:00 pm. We got a motel in Frostburg and then met in a room. We were smudged, smoked the pipe, and had a talking circle. We were happy and thankful because we had covered around 90 miles including about 50 miles through the mountains and had felt strong. We then went to dinner at an Italian restaurant; we laughed because Don ordered a pizza for himself. Some people washed their clothes, some relaxed in the hot tub. Sue, Tyra and Tyra's son Colten arrived around 8:30 pm.

Nov. 25—Day 15 (Wednesday) Frostburg to Frederick, Maryland

Ceremony started before sunrise in parking lot behind motel in Frostburg, Maryland. Thanked Gary for sharing a teaching the previous night. Gary had told us that there was a time when humans had lost their way and so the Creator was going to destroy the earth and start over. Migizi pleaded with the Creator for a chance to find just one person who was still living according to the Creator's original instructions. The Creator gave Migizi until sunrise and said if such a person could be found then humans wouldn't be destroyed. Migizi flew all night searching the earth without finding anyone. But just at the last moment before sunrise Migizi found one old Anishinaabe couple in front of their lodge by a fire following the original instructions. And so Migizi immediately flew straight up crying out four times to the Creator that someone had been found. With this the Creator gave humans another chance.

All 15 runners and walkers plus the 3 staffs were smudged. The sun and the morning colors rose in a low area between two hills. Gary said that if Migizi were looking for someone this morning he would see all of us, and our hearts were touched and glad. Today we were asked to pray for the women, the strength of our nations. Sue & Tyra joined us the previous night and were now part of the circle.

Drove to just before Frostburg and to the top of Big Savage Mountain at 2900 feet. Continued running down the National Road and passed the first tollgate house. Ran through Cumberland and somehow all of us mistakenly took Williams Road which turned out to be a wonderful mistake. This road went up Warrior Mountain, through an orchard at the top, wound down through a valley surrounded by trees, fields, and a stream for about 15 miles before coming out in Flintstone. We saw many animals and birds and had a special feeling like this valley was alive and somehow blessed. Prayers were sent to the White Buffalo Calf Woman. Eleven horses were seen in this valley, a reminder of the 11 walkers/runners in the core team. Gene flushed a turkey. Runners stopped on a wooded downhill corner and played throwing rocks for awhile trying to hit a small sign.

The road then turned into a series of long rather steep uphill stretches followed by equally long downhill stretches. Joel and Don ran their miles up Sideline Hill which crested near some radio towers. Gary ran uphill for 1.5 miles before reaching the top of Green Ridge mountain; he heard crickets chirping, saw a pileated woodpecker, and saw hawks crying out above the staff. The sky once again is blue and the temperature warm. The weather is wonderful to run in. This good weather seems to be following us and we feel blessed. Around the top of another mountain the bird nations formed a "kettle," a formation we were told they assume before their migration begins. At first we only noticed a few birds but as we looked we saw that there were perhaps 30-40 circling like smoke rising. As we continued to watch we saw more bird-nations flying over the tree tops to join the circle. Hawks, golden eagles, osprey, and buzzards were seen.

We took Highway 68 which was a cutacross and took us around Hagerstown. We noticed rows of fieldstones piled up like fences along the road. Some fields weren't picked of their stones and the long rocks seemed to be like a spine of mother earth made visible. The road shoulder became very narrow and more and more treacherous as it became darker and the holiday traffic increased. We were hoping to run up South Mountain and to Frederick but decided to quit shortly after dark.

We drove to the next town & waited for all the runners and walkers before following Sue's huge green truck to Frederick & the Quaker house. We were smudged, smoked the pipe, and had a talking circle in their meeting room. About 30-40 Quakers sat silently in the room watching in what seemed to be a tolerant and respectful way. We then gathered in a large circle in their kitchen and held hands before lining up to fill our plates.

After dinner we once again gathered in the meeting room so that the Quakers could have a "moment of silence." We were told that this would usually last about 15-30 minutes; people would sit silently until someone would share a thought or feeling; then people would sit for 2-3 minutes in silence and contemplation before someone else might share something new.

The silence, the warmth of the room, the long day of activity, and the feeling of being full created a relaxed and sleepy atmosphere. After about 10 minutes no one had yet spoken. About this time Jim let out a couple of fairly heavy breaths. Neil who had been resting his head on the chair in front of him, glanced over when he heard this sound. He immediately became alarmed when he saw that Jim had fallen asleep because he was sure that some pretty loud snoring was going to start in another breath or two. He quickly leaned over several chairs and tried to gently poke Jim in his side. However, rather than wake up silently, Jim woke up with a start and blurted out a noise that sort of sounded like "what." At the same time he half-lunged at Neil who jerked back in surprise. All of the runners immediately began exercising every bit of self-control to stifle their laughter. Bodies shook and faces were either hung down or hidden behind hats. After about a minute, Brook couldn't contain herself any longer and let out a laugh followed by a shorter one a few seconds later. A few minutes later a Quaker lady spoke up and said how nice the laughter sounded and thanked Brook for sharing it. Another lady spoke up a couple minutes later and remarked how nice it was to hear some of the runners say that it was a pretty good day and commented that we don't hear people say that often. After the "moment of silence" ended everyone introduced themselves. When Jim said his name was Sleepy the dwarf everyone let out what remained of the laughter they had held in.

Nov. 26—Day 16 (Thursday) Frederick, Maryland to Clarksburg, Maryland

We rose slowly. Most of the runners wanted to cover a few miles today so around 9:30 am they left. About five hours later they returned and had covered almost 40 miles and reached Clarksburg only 25 miles or so from D.C. Several people drove to a Quaker camp in the mountains and looked for a place to have a sweat. We found one but because of the amount of work needed and nighttime being so close, we decided not to have one. Around 4 pm Thanksgiving dinner was served; after dinner Jim gave the Quakers a birch bark basket, some tobacco ties, wild rice, hats, shirts, and Mille Lacs pins. He gave the lady who had spoken about Brooks laughter a t-shirt.

Nov. 27—Day 17 (Friday) Frederick, Maryland to Washington, DC.

We rose around 7:00 and had a ceremony in the Quaker house living room. Tobasonakwut had arrived the day before, and we smoked his pipe in the morning after being smudged. Gary gave us an eagle feather that he had been asked to present. We had what turned out to be our last talking circle; Neil and Gene were overwhelmed with emotion and everyone hugged each other afterwards. We drove to Clarksburg and asked Budman, Eva, and Erik to run with all three staffs for the first mile. Budman's mother, Thelma, joined our caravan for awhile. Other runners and walkers accompanied each other during the next few hours. Gary found a freshly killed turkey vulture and gave most everyone a feather. As we got closer to D.C. it became more difficult and tricky to find parking spots every mile. Pow-wow music was constantly playing and people were dancing and singing wherever we were stopped and waiting for runners.

We soon found ourselves in Georgetown heading down Wisconsin street. After a couple of miles Erik took the staff from Neil & sprinted off down the sidewalk. The vehicles got going right away but it was like a beehive; traffic was slow & people were everywhere shopping and sightseeing. Erik disappeared into the crowd but we figured, like always, we'd catch up and find the runner in a few blocks. We drove about a 1/2 mile before Wisconsin Street ended at a "T"; Water Street had very little traffic and because it was nearly deserted we couldn't help but think that we might have made a wrong turn. We started down Water Street anyway thinking that Erik must have gone this way and we'd see him up ahead. After about a 1/2 mile we ran into the downtown area not too far from the White House. We still hadn't seen Erik so we started backtracking; when we did this, Gary who had slipped several blocks behind in traffic got separated from us. After about 15 minutes of driving back into Georgetown and looking down Water Street, we decided that we weren't going to find Erik. He was on his own and we hoped he would go to the Supreme Court like we had previously discussed. Everyone except Gary had a cell phone in their vehicle and so after a few calls we agreed to meet there.

We gradually found the Supreme Court and parking spots nearby. We walked to the Supreme Court and began congregating. Erik hadn't arrived so Neil decided to start walking back in hopes of finding him. After about 15 minutes he noticed Erik walking near the pool on the west side of the Congressional building. They were glad to see each other, shook hands, and ran back the 1/2 mile or so to the Supreme Court steps. We had reached our destination and accomplished what we had set out to do. We had planned to walk the last mile together so we were all a little discombobulated when the run ended so unexpectedly.

Later, Erik said that when he saw Water Street he reacted like the rest of us and wasn't sure which way to go so he popped into a store to get directions. It was during those 2-3 seconds that our caravan drove by. Erik said he saw us go by and began running down the street behind us trying to get our attention but we were looking ahead for him. He never caught us before we sped up and got into the downtown part of town. Gary found Erik and was able to stay with him until the White House but when he went to find a parking spot, he got stuck in traffic.

Gary never hooked back up with the group & after circling the Supreme Court building after the rest of us had already left, and then fighting traffic around the Vietnam Veterans Memorial, he decided to head back. Randy also had become separated from the group in Georgetown; he got out of Gene and Eva's van at a gas station and they left thinking he had jumped in the white van. Jim saw Randy a little while later and told him to hop in Sue's truck and he did. When told about this later at the Supreme Court, his brother became very and openly angry at Jim. Jim decided it was time to head back home and did so. Eva & Gene checked into a Quaker house and left the next morning. The Trickster had waited until the very end; we were taught and reminded that we need to be continually on guard against his mischief, distractions, and disruptions.

APPENDIX B
The Mikwendaagoziwag Run

Sandy Lake, Minnesota to Madeline Island
December 2-4, 2000

CORE RUNNERS

Timothy Arnold	Elizabeth Martin	Margaret Schlender
Archie Cash	John Mojica	Joel Schaugobay
Sue Erickson	Larry Nesper	Nick Van Der Puy
Don Graves	Charlie Rasmussen	Graham Zorn
Neil Kmiecik	Jenny Schlender	Jim Zorn
Sandy Lyon	Jim Schlender	

PARTICIPANTS

Carson Ackley	Garaka Dveorakova	Robert Van Zile
Fred Ackley	Bob Jackson	Jeannie Sue Van Zile
Howard Bichler	Lorraine Norrgard	Lydia Vitort
Russell Boyd	Ernie St. Germaine	Rachal Zorn
Peter David	Josh Van Zile	

MADELINE ISLAND FIREKEEPERS

Richard Jack	Francis Leoso	Butch Stone
		Gilmore Wilson

Graphics

ACHS Aitkin County Historical Society

AM Amoose Moore

BE Bruce Edwards, *Flint Journal*

BT Bucko Teeple

BRPL Bad River Public Library

COR Charlie Otto Rasmussen

DB Dick Bancroft

EC Esteban Chiriboga

FK Francis Kmiecik

GLIFWC Great Lakes Indian Fish & Wildlife Commission image

JG Jonathan Gilbert

JS Jim Schlender

JZ Jim Zorn

SE Sue Erickson

SW Steve White

WHI Wisconsin Historical Society

Works Cited

Aitkin Independent Age
September 27, 2000: "Brief and Tragic History of the Sandy Lake Indian Agency."

Armstrong, Benjamin G. "Reminiscences of Life Among the Chippewas," [1892] ed. William Converse Haygood.*Wisconsin Magazine of History,* 55 (Summer 1972).

Bieder, Robert, ed. Kohl, Johann Georg. *Kitchi-Gami: Life Among the Lake Superior Ojibway [1860],* St. Paul: Minnesota Historical Society Press, 1985.

Buffalo to Lea (November 6, 1851), in United States District Court, District of Minnesota, Fourth Division, Plaintiff's Exhibit: P-0073, 226-231.

Buffalohead, Roger and Priscilla. *Against the Tide of American History: The Story of the Mille Lacs Anishinabe.* Cass Lake Minn.: The Minnesota Chippewa Tribe, 1985.

Cleland, Charles E. *The Place of the Pike (Gnoozhekaaning): A History of the Bay Mills Indian Community.* Ann Arbor: University of Michigan Press, 2001.

Cleland, Charles E. *The Rites of Conquest.* Ann Arbor: University of Michigan Press, 1992.

Clifton, James A. "Wisconsin Death March: Explaining the Extremes in Old Northwest Indian Removal." *Transactions of the Wisconsin Academy of Sciences, Arts and Letters* 75.

Danziger, Edmund Jefferson Jr. *The Chippewas of Lake Superior.* Norman: University of Oklahoma Press, 1979.

Deloria, Vine Jr. *Custer Died for Your Sins.* Norman: University of Oklahoma Press, 1969.

Diedrich, Mark. *Ojibway Oratory.* Rochester, Minn.: Coyote Books, 1990.

Fox, Stephen. *The American Conservation Movement: John Muir and His Legacy.* Madison: University of Wisconsin Press, 1981.

Frederick News-Post
November 27, 1998 "Tribe on thousand mile quest: stops and prays in Frederick."

Fritzen, John. "Portages & Old Trails Inland and Adjacent to Jay Cooke State Park: St. Louis River Grand Portage," 1935. Fifteen-page typescript.

Great Lakes Indian Fish & Wildlife Commission. *A Guide to Understanding Ojibwe Treaty Rights,* October 1999.

_____"Waabanong Run financial report." One-page unpublished document reporting donations and expenses.

Hibbing Daily Tribune
March 14, 1993: "Mille Lacs settlement backer charges racism in some critics."

Holbrook, Arthur Tenny. "Antione Dennis: Last of the Chippewa Mail Runners," *Wisconsin Magazine of History,* 22 (June 1939).

Institute for the Development of Indian Law, "Treaties and Agreements of the Chippewa Indians." Oklahoma City: Oklahoma City University Law School, n.d.

Kmiecik, Neil and Jim Schlender. "Sketch of Running Route by Day: Waabanong Run" Online publication: www.glifwc.org: 1998.

Lurie, Nancy Oestreich. *Wisconsin Indians.* Revised. Madison: The State Historical Society of Wisconsin, 2002.

Masinaigan
Special Edition, Dec. 1983: "Task force state reach pact;"
    "Fish & Wildlife Commission proposed."
July 1984: "The Voigt Decision raises concerns."
Fall 1990: "Long distance run seeks peace, spiritual healing."
Winter 1997: "First treaty harvest underway in Minnesota 1837 ceded territory."
Winter 1998-99: "Treaty rights on trial once again."
Spring 1999: "Whichever way the court rules."
Supplement Edition, Spring 1999: "The Waabanong Run from Wisconsin to D.C."

Michigan Department of Natural Resources. "Landmark Dates," printed copy of online data provided by the Department February 14, 2002.

Mille Lacs Messenger
April 22, 1992: "Heated words exchanged at the Capitol rally."
January 6, 1993: "Messenger Mailbag: No one should give up their rights."
January 27, 1993: "DNR and Band unveil the details."
February 24, 1993: "Nothing is certain about Band's vote."
March 10, 1993: "Mille Lacs Band gives a thumbs up to settlement."

Minnesota Historical Society. Chippewa Annuity Roll, Nov. 28, 1850, M390, Reel 1. Microfilm copy of original in National Archives, Record Group 75.

Nabokov, Peter. *Indian Running: Native American History & Tradition,* Santa Fe: Ancient City Press, 1981.

Neill, Rev. Edward Duffield, *The History of Minnesota from the Earliest French Explorations to the Present Time,* Fourth ed., revised. Minneapolis: Minnesota Historical Company, 1882.

Nesbit, Robert C., and William F. Thompson. *Wisconsin: A History.* 2nd revised ed. Madison: University of Wisconsin Press.

News from Indian Country
Late Feb. 2000, "She was born white, and they named her Miracle."

New Ulm Journal
February 10, 1993: "DNR, Mille Lacs officials outline pact."

Oberly, James W. *The Lake Superior Chippewas and Treaty Rights in the Ceded Territory of Wisconsin: Population, Prices, Land, Natural Resources, and Regulation, 1837-1983.* Unpublished manuscript, 1991.

Outdoor News [Minnesota edition]
April 24, 1992: "Capital rally sends message."
January 11, 2002: "Outdoor Insights."
January 18, 2002: "DNR says no observers at state-tribal meeting."

Outdoor News [Wisconsin edition]
December 18, 1999: "Wisconsin AG, Crist differ on High Court's comments."

Pitezel, John H. *Lights and Shades of Missionary Life: Containing Travels, Sketches, Incidents, and Missionary Efforts, During Nine Years Spent in the Region of Lake Superior.* Cincinnati: Western Book Concern, R. P. Thompson, Printer, 1859.

Pfaff, Tim. *Paths of the People: The Ojibwe in the Chippewa Valley.* Eau Claire, WI: Chippewa Valley Museum Press, 1993.

Proper Economic Resource Management [PERM] Newsletter
"Position Paper." n.d.
_____. January 2000

Rapid City Journal
Dec. 29, 1990, "Big Foot Ride fulfills dream."

Rasmussen, Charlie Otto. Personal Journal, July 28, 1998 to April 2, 1999, unpublished journal in possession of author.

_____. *Where the River is Wide: Pahquahwong and the Chippewa Flowage.* Odanah, WI: Great Lakes Indian Fish & Wildlife Commission Press, 1998.

Ryser, Rudolf C. "Anti-Indian Movement on the Tribal Frontier," Occasional Paper #16. Olympia, Wash.: Center for World Indigenous Studies, 1992.

St. Cloud Times
March 13, 1993: "Treaty foes to Senate Panel: Vote 'no'."

Satz, Ronald N. *Chippewa Treaty Rights: The Reserved Rights of Wisconsin's Chippewa Indians in Historical Perspective.* 2nd printing, revised. Madison: University of Wisconsin Press for the Wisconsin Academy of Sciences, Arts, and Letters, 1994.

Smith, Elbert B. *The Presidencies of Zachary Taylor & Millard Fillmore.* Lawrence: The University Press of Kansas, 1988.

United States Department of the Interior. *Casting Light Upon the Waters: A Joint Fishery Assessment of the Wisconsin Ceded Territory.* 2nd Edition, 1993.

Upham, Warren. *Minnesota Place Names: A Geographic Encyclopedia.* 3rd ed. Revised, Minnesota Historical Society Press: St. Paul, 2001.

Warren, William W. *History of the Ojibway People.* Reprint edition, Minnesota Historical Society Press: St. Paul, 1984.

Whaley, Rick with Walter Bresette. *Walleye Warriors.* New Society Publishers: Philadelphia, 1994.

White, Bruce M., "The Regional Context of the Removal Order of 1850," in *Fish in the Lakes, Wild Rice, and Game in Abundance* (James M. McClurken, compiler). East Lansing: Michigan State University Press, 2000.

Winton, E. Ward, and Kay Brown Winton, eds., "Memoirs of Ward Winton: Legal Battles in Behalf of the Lac Court[e] Oreilles Band of Chippewa Indians of Wisconsin, 1972," in *Historical Collections of Washburn County and the Surrounding Indianhead Country,* 2 vols. Shell Lake: Washburn Co. Historical Society, 1980.

Legal Documents

Lac Courte Oreilles Band of Lake Superior Chippewa Indians, et. al v. State of Wisconsin, et al.
–Deposition of James Pipe Mustache, June 28, 1990 (Docket #1593)

Lac du Flambeau v. Stop Treaty Abuse-Wisconsin, 759 F. Supp. 1339 (W.D. Wis. 1991)

Lac du Flambeau v. Stop Treaty Abuse-Wisconsin, 991F. 2d 1249 (7th Cir. 1993)

Mille Lacs v. Minnesota, 861 F.Supp. 784 (D.Minn. 1994)

Mille Lacs v. Minnesota, Civil No. 3-94-1226
–Declaration of David H. Getches in Support of Bands' Attorneys' Fee Petition.

Minnesota v. Mille Lacs, 119 S.Ct. 1187 (1999)

Minnesota v. Mille Lacs (97-1337) 124 F.3d 904.

Minnesota v. Mille Lacs (97-1337)
–Official Transcript, Supreme Court of the United States.

Minnesota v. Mille Lacs (97-1337)
–Brief for respondents Bad River Band of Lake Superior Chippewa Indians and Lac du Flambeau Band of Lake Superior Chippewa Indians.

People of Michigan v. Jondreau, 384 Mich. 539, 185 N. W 2d 375 (1971)

People of Michigan v. LeBlanc, 248 N.W. 2d 199 (1976)

State of Wisconsin v. Gurnoe, 53 Wis. 2d 390 (1972)

Personal Interviews

Benton, Eddie interview by author at Lac Courte Oreilles, January 22, 1998.

Hockings, Nick telephone interview by author, October 21, 1999.

Kinew, Tobasonakwut interview by author at Odanah, WI, November 4, 1999.

Kmiecik, Neil interview by author at Odanah, WI, October 28, 2001.

Lac Courte Oreilles Waabanong Runners, interview by author at Reserve, WI, February 19, 1999.

Mille Lacs Waabanong Runners, interview by author at Mille Lacs, MN, March 19, 1999.

Tribble, Mike interview by author at Reserve, WI, October 5, 2001.

St. Croix Waabanong Runners, interview by author at Hertel, WI, September 28, 1999.

Walking Elk, Mitch telephone interview by author, December 10, 1999.

Wedll, Don, interview at Mille Lacs, MN by author, November 14, 2001.